DREAM BOATS
AND
OTHER STORIES

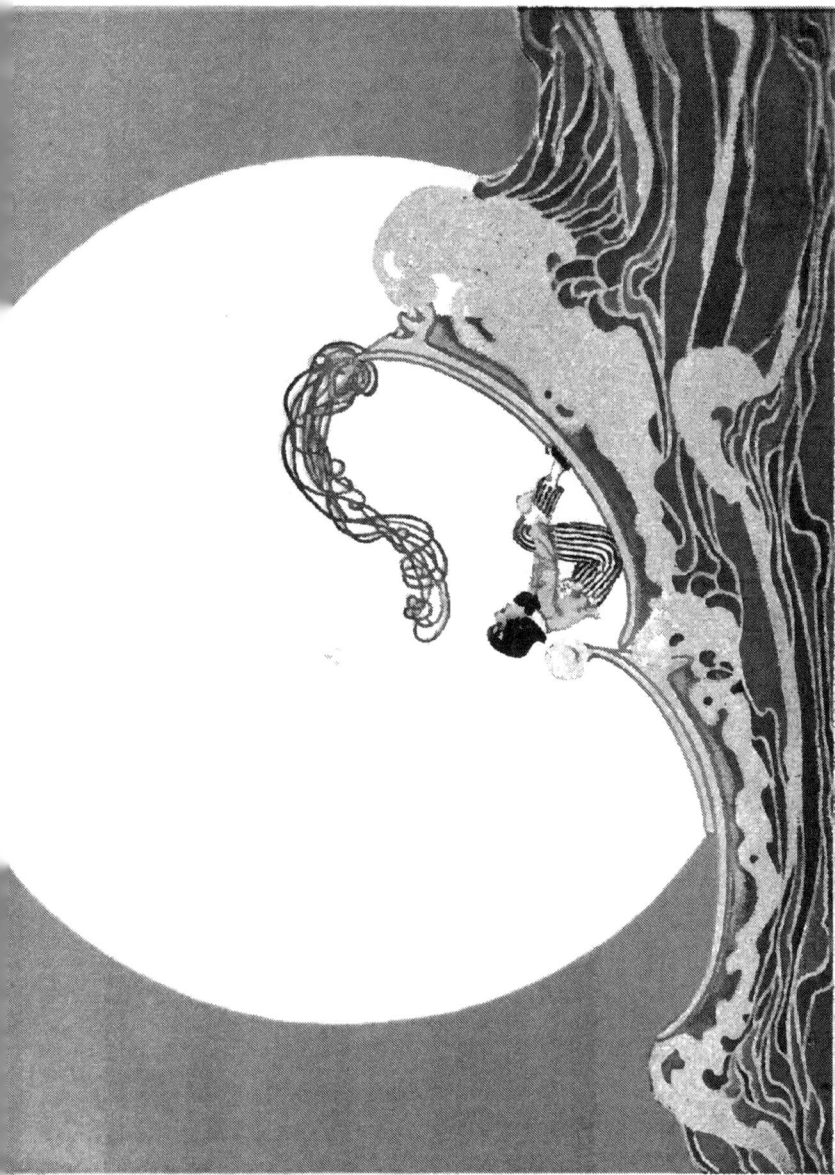

"SHE · TIED · MY · BOAT · TO · THE · NORTH · STAR · SO · I · WOULD · NOT ·

·DREAM·BOATS·

·AND·OTHER·STORIES·

·PORTRAITS·AND·HISTORIES·OF·FAUNS·FAIRIES·FISHES·
·AND·OTHER·PLEASANT·CREATURES·

·BY·

·DUGALD·STEWART·WALKER·

·ILLUSTRATOR·OF·
·ANDERSEN'S·FAIRY·TALES·

·GARDEN·CITY·   ·NEW·YORK·
·DOUBLEDAY·PAGE·AND·COMPANY·
1920

·TO·
·DAVID·
·MY·FATHER·

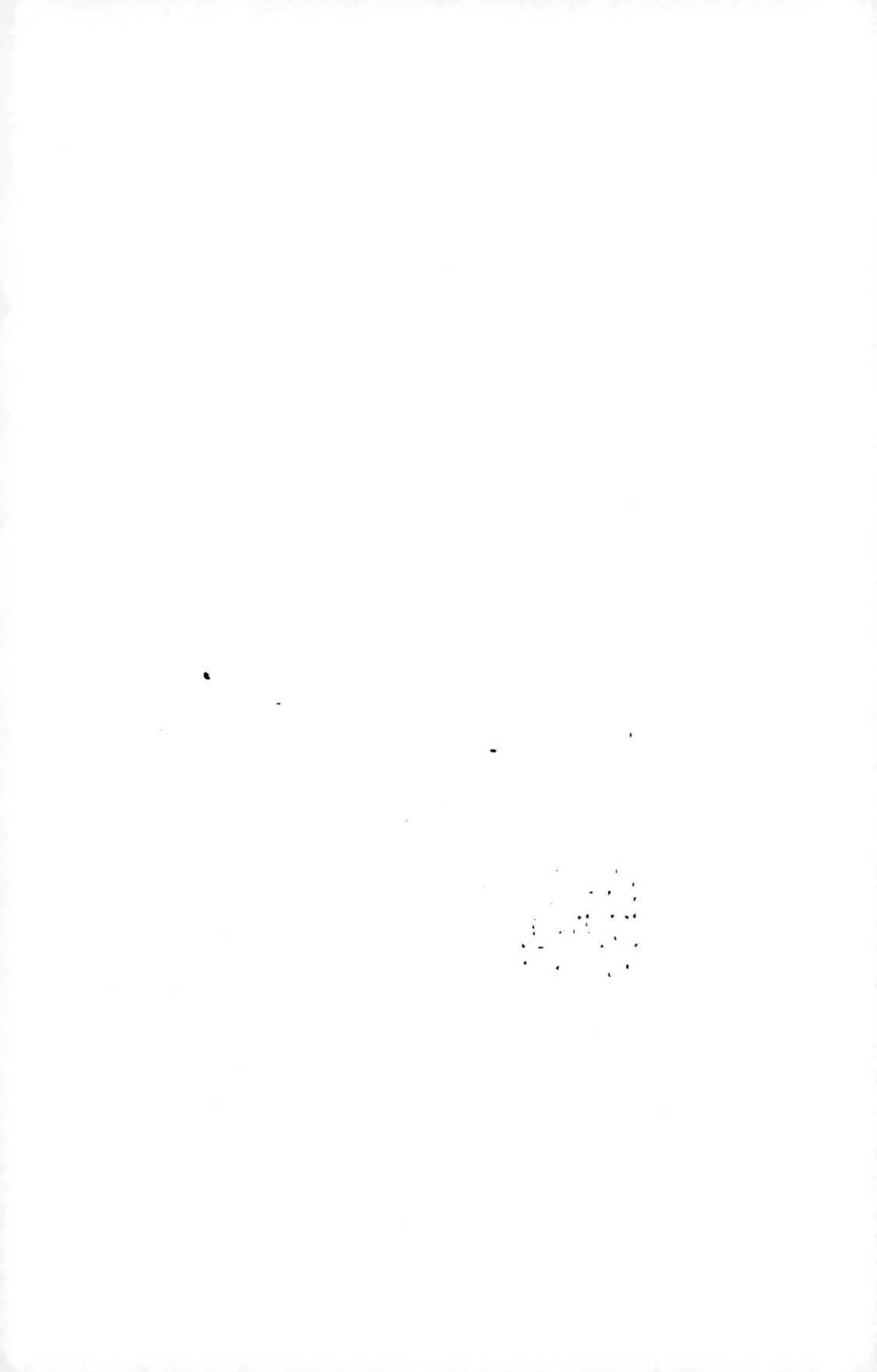

THE SUNLIT SEA

A FOREWORD

THERE is a far-away blue sea of unending wonder and belief. A fragile craft is launched from a Mother's arms, upon its waters. You are the helmsman of the vessel and you are the guardian.

Safely through tempests and gales and over stretches of Sunlit waters you must pilot the ship. The path is strewn with icebergs, wreckage and many boats making for the same harbour. All the little ships make their trial voyage through the white-capped, dancing waves of "Let's Play" and "Let's Pretend".

Back into the bay of youth, where lies the haven of a Mother's arms, each little vessel will drift if the pilot does not stupidly keep his wheel turned to the point on the compass that reads *Grow-up-*

South by *As-fast-as-you-can-East.* The craft laden with a cargo, that is your heart, will surely return to the pleasant waters of youth unless you are grown up so high you cannot become as a little child.

If you wish, and wish with all your heart, you can come to join us in our play, which in honour of the waves of "Let's Pretend", through which I hope your little craft has passed, I have called "Dream Boats."

CONTENTS

PICTURES

IN COLOUR

HISTORIES

STORKS

HUSH! Hush! At night when the lonely call of the whippoorwills made the marsh creep nearer than the other side of the meadow, Ruth Jane Crutchfield, the nurse, lay down on the bed beside David's little boy. She told him about the storks that bring children and leave them among the ferns and the alder bushes back there in the marshes.

As soon as the whippoorwills ceased calling, the spell broke, and the marsh returned again beyond the meadow where Cherry, the Jersey cow, lived.

As the nurse's footsteps faded away in the dark hall, David crept out of his bed and stole into mine and came close to me because it was a cold night.

In a whisper he said, said he: "But where do the storks get 'em?"

And I said, said I: "They come from away up behind the stars, where the Spring comes from. Up there, sits One—(I can't remember much about her, only that she made me think of a dewdrop—not such a dewdrop as you and I can see, but a dewdrop if it were as large as the whole world)—and all the children are in her lap.

"Each one has a little harness made of ribbon. And there are faun babies, and fairy babies, and baby babies. The fauns' harness is purple like grapes, and the fairies' is silver like bubbles in moonlight, and the babies' is just pink and blue; and that's how the stork knows which is which.

"Now, the storks fly up there (it's wonderful the distance storks can fly, isn't it?) and each one takes a baby in his beak by the loop at the top of the harness. Down he starts, and all the way down the baby practises kicking.

"But before they start, the One who is like what a dewdrop would be if it were as large as the whole world, gives to each baby a dandelion.

· "UP · THERE, · SITS · ONE— · I · CAN'T · REMEMBER · MUCH ·
· ABOUT · HER" ·

And she says, says she: 'When you reach the lowest circle of stars this dandelion will have gone to seed. Then you must blow on it and see what time you will be born.'

"So when they come to the lowest circle of stars, *puff*, *puff*, blow all the babies on the dandelions which have gone to seed, to see when they will be born. This is a very important matter. But the down of the dandelion sometimes gets into the storks' eyes and as they haven't any memory to speak of, they make sad mistakes in the places where they leave the babies. Sometimes fairies are left with people, and sometimes even fauns—though of that I am not quite sure."

POLLEN PEOPLE

Balsam, Sweet Basil, and Gold Buttercup

IN LITTLE villages of gaily painted pavilions live the golden people of the dusty pollen. Every house is set on a fragile stem, swaying back and forth as if waving a welcome to all flying things. Sometimes at the approach of storms they shield the doorway with a silken awning, thus protecting the countless family from loss by wind and rain. They are very proud of the names of their houses. And have they not a right to be?

Acacia, Anemone, Azalia, and Amaryllis

The children are brought up in most exclusive fashion, straying not beyond the petaled threshold before they have been formally introduced. Living close to their mothers, they think of another pollen child who is near its mother, roaming in

6

the fields of that dream a child has when its mother is near.

Oh, dream one dream for me, ye little star-faced children of a love that endures unto the end!

Lily, Labernum, Larkspur, and Queen Anne's Lace

Sometimes the houses introduce their children with a prolonged feast of nectar. Painted in bright colours, they exhale invitations of fragrance to their dearly loved friends, the bees. The guests arrive humming their exquisite song of labour and cease not to sing while they partake of the feast of honey. Departing, they avow their thankfulness, taking with them the pollen children who desire to go forth to seek their fortunes.

Lupin, Lavender, and Laurel

Again at night other houses present their children with parties of pale yellow and white, that passers by may be attracted even in the darkest night.

Primroses, Evening Glory, and the Moonflower Vine

While others scatter their invitations broadcast, and as the night advances over the earth, the welcoming fragrance increases, thus luring to their feast many coloured moths.

Hyacinth, Heliotrope, and Mignonette

And some give dances exclusively for the wind, dimly lighted parties-where no refreshments are served. Each guest is given charge of a pollen child, that the child may later be carried to a distant meadow where it may build a fragrant village of its own.

Petunia, Robin's Plantain, and the wild, Wild Phlox

From early Spring until the Indian Summer, there are innumerable little parties, each one a

· " IN · THE · COMMONPLACE · CORNERS · OF · THE · EARTH ·
· THERE · MAY · BE · A · PAIR · OF · POLLEN · LOVERS " ·

festival for the exquisite purpose of sending forth the children to find the unchanging one who is to be the comrade in life's dearest adventure.

Oleander, Cape Jasmine, Iris, and Columbine

Therefore in the commonplace corners of the earth they have their sweet romances, meeting and recognizing the one they will cherish all the days of their lives.

Sweet William, Snapdragon, and Shepherd's Purse

Here you see a picture of a pair of pollen lovers—first-born of the ancient house of forget-me-not.

On a cobweb suspended from a string-bean vine (that we chop down and eat for our dinner), the lovers have found a trysting place at the rising of the moon.

O Lady's Slipper, Fuchsia, Verbena, and Rue

"Co loo—co loo. I love you! Do, do, do," says he, her lover, to her. And she, his sweetheart, replies to him: "Co coo to lu—Co coo to lu. I love you! Too, too, too."

They do not blush save as trees blush in the springtime, when in their veins flows the sap of innumerable flowers.

Ring all your little bells, O Bluebells, Canterbury Bells, and bells of the Solomon's Seal.

After the wedding, they settle in a seed. And life is a long adventure of bud and leaf and bloom. Thus in the renewal of themselves in other flowers, they live happily for ever and ever and ever.

Myrtle, Mimosa, Magnolia, and Marigold

"AND · PIPE · THE · LITTLE · SONGS · THAT · ARE · INSIDE · OF · BUBBLES

SECOND TEETH

FAUNS and fairies and fishes do not shed their first teeth and so they cannot shed their youth and joy.

Babies do shed their first teeth because they know that second teeth will come, and nearly always in this distracting adventure they make mistakes and shed both their youth and joy. But now and then a baby will not shed his youth and joy until his second teeth are firmly rooted. It is these delightful creatures who can balance on a fish's nose and pipe the little songs that are in the bursting bubbles of the foam.

If there are not songs inside of bubbles, what is in them?

THE BLOOMING OF A FAIRY
BABY

ALL the pleasantest creatures that inhabit the worlds of wind and earth and water, enter those worlds in a shell of some sort.

In a stream the mother Dragon Fly leaves her precious treasure, where the sun, shining through the water, keeps the little eggs as warm as they should be. The mother Butterfly places her eggs under the leaves of the food plant upon which the baby caterpillar, after it is hatched, is destined to live. And the mother Butterfly always chooses the right plant. In a nest of cobwebs, moss, and down, the mother bird keeps her eggs warm with the feathers of her breast. And thus it is with alligators, toads, and lizards, turtles, fish, bugs, and snakes, and all the creatures with which one can be so friendly.

When the moon is on the wane, the mother Fairy strings her eggs, which are dew drops, on a strand of cobweb suspended from the sweetest flower. She only ruffles the feathers in her wings, preens herself, and sits as still as any star watching and waiting for a lovely thing to happen. When the moon has set, and the stars have followed after with their fading lights, the winged mother's patient waiting is rewarded, for all that is needed to bring forth the miracle of a dew-shell is the image of a star reflected in its shining surface all through the summer night.

Then each fairy baby lifts its head and opens its eyes very wide to see what will happen (and sticks out its lower lip, in case it should be something dreadful). But a baby fairy thinks it is very funny to see the stars set, so it laughs at the declining lights. The sweetness of its laughter breaks the dewdrop, and it enters into the world smiling, and can never cease to be joyful all the days of its life.

Sometimes, though not very often, they stop laughing long enough to drink the dew which has been the little reticule of beauty to bring them from that world to this.

Of course, there are some dewdrops that do not hatch, for a strangely sweet and subtle reason known only to the fairy inside. Perhaps they think it is pleasanter to live within a pearl strung on a string around a lovely lady's neck, than to be a whimsical creature who goes through life seeking to find what prettily illogical thing it can do next.

MOULTING

WHEN you see a fairy flying through the air as though he did not care a winkle where he went, you may know he doesn't. He possesses a pair of horns which are better than another pair of eyes or an entirely new nose. Indeed, who can say but that gossamer stringed music may reach the fairy's heart through these same horns? How else would he hear the melody of the moonlight?

When fairies are hatched, they have small, flaccid horns and limp wings. In order to work up the circulation of colour through the veins of the wings and into the tips of the horns, they must have exercise.

Attaching themselves to leaves, head down and feet up, and hanging pendant, the newly hatched fairies fan the air with their wings.

When the wings and horns are spread, then the greatest moment in a fairy's whole lifetime arrives. On airy pinions this creature, which has apparently been sleeping the sleep of the dead in its dewdrop eggshell, flies aloft into the air, the playmate of sunlight and thistledown, star dust and moonshine.

Now, instead of second teeth, the fairies get second horns. They haven't any one to tie a string around the first horns to jerk them out. So they butt into a flower, and pull and pull and pull. That much done, they go away, leaving their old horns sticking in one of the petals.

After the close of this adventure of horn shedding, called moulting, they attach themselves firmly to a twig, feet up, there waiting for new horns to grow down. For, you must surely know, nothing about fairies ever *grows up*.

THE GODMOTHER BUSH

THERE are seven fairy frigates that will not sail forth to-night on the airy seas from the port of a thistle pod.

These I have captured and as I let them drift from my open window I will blow a wish upon them for seven different mothers whom I know, and though you might not believe it, one of these mothers is a mother bird.

It may seem strange that a thistle seed has power to carry wishes to the fairies. But it is not, and I am about to tell you why.

In the land of the fairies, that lies so near and yet beyond the vision of men's eyes, fairy mothers do not have nursemaids with whom to leave their babies when they needs must fly away to do all those things mothers have to do; the things that take so long—so long. Therefore, they make friends with spiders and ask them to spin webs in the bushes whereon there are thorns.

When a web is spun a mother lays her baby in it. There the baby is safe, for the thorns keep all enemy creatures away.

Before the mother leaves, she gives her baby the new moon for a plaything, and lying in the cradle, he plays and plays with the crescent rattle until it is turned upside down and the water spills out. "That is why it rains to-morrow!"

You can make wishes for mothers come true only on those seven thistle seeds gathered from the friendly bush that has played nursemaid to the mother of a little fairy.

If you desire to make a wish for your mother or for some one else's mother (for it is almost, but not quite, as sweet to send a wish for another's mother as it is to wish for one's own,) gather seven thistle seeds from a bush wherein there is a spider's web. Give them to seven

· "WHY · IT · RAINS · TOMORROW" ·

children. After they have said "God bless
Mother" on a night when there is a new moon,
let each child open the window, just so high, but
not high enough to fall out; make a wish; blow
the thistle seed into the night. It will journey,
as a special envoy, to a port on the sea of air
where the fairies live, and there deliver your
message. The fairies will make it come true.

Maybe after the sweet errand is over, the seed
will remember that it bears also the promise of a
thistle as a precious cargo, and, casting off its
anchor, steadfastly sail to some barren road side,
where next summer another child will gather
from it seven more seeds that will sail forth on a
like quest.

You must not tell the wish you have made and
you must not ask the fairies to send your mother
a diamond dog-collar or an aëroplane. The
fairies do not know about these things. You
might wish that some one would toss her a
flower; perhaps she would like to hear music,

and maybe it would be nice for her to sit in the sunshine for an hour. These I can assure you are the real gifts of the fairies. But in order to have them bestowed upon the rightful mother, remember, you must open your window only *so wide;* and don't fall out.

BUTTERFLY'S NIGHTMARE

MOTHS are cousins to the fairies, once removed, on their fathers' side, for they are on the wing between the dusk of evening and the twilight of early morning. Butterflies are cousins to the fairies, twice removed, on their mothers' side, because they fly when the sun is up, and the lights are shining bright in dewdrops.

The fairies are friendly with their first cousins, and with their second cousins too, but they can live on more intimate terms with butterflies since they are not on the wing at the same time. For when they are flying, they are so busy foraging for a dinner, that they cannot pause to pass the time of day.

Striking family resemblances are often seen in the markings and patterns on fairies' and moths' and butterflies' wings.

In the Dream-time, when the birds have ruffled their feathers and put their heads under their wings, all things may be found. Every dainty butterfly maiden is swayed to dreams by gentle winds on her sweet, bubble-like bed of a downy, dandelion seed-ball, so feathery, soft, and sweet. Butterflies eat the honey and pollen that are held within the chalice of flowers. But just as there are human beings who eat dinners that they should not, so are there butterflies who, try as hard as they may, cannot resist a tempting meal of the pollen of snapdragons, cowslips, toad-flax, or one of the irresistible dishes so tempting to a butterfly's palate.

And so, all through a summer night, two fairies keep watch with outstretched arms under every butterfly's bed, lest by chance the sleeper has indulged in a dinner of the pollen that gives one nightmare. And if, perhaps, some late straying wind desires to learn the time of night and suddenly blows her bed in bits of drifting

· "LEST · A · NIGHTMARE · SHOULD · COME · TO ·THE · FAIRIES' ·
· COUSIN · TWICE · REMOVED · ON · THEIR · MOTHER'S · SIDE" ·

down from under her dreaming self, the two fairies are there, waiting and prepared to catch that cousin, twice removed, on their mother's side.

BAD CHILDREN

FAIRY children are never bad until they have cut their first teeth, and no one knows that they are bad then except their mother. She thinks it is a pretty thing, but she pretends she doesn't. If she had a corner, she would stand them in it. As she has none, she takes each naughty child's chin in her hand, very gently, and says:

"Child, you have lost your nose. Go look for it. And if you don't stick you finger in the hole where your nose used to be, until you find it, you will find a Gold Nose at the same time."

Now, the fairies never think. For, if they did, they would see that they would have no use for a Gold Nose even if they found one. So, before they stop to think, off sails each naughty fairy up into the air to look for its nose, with its hands for oars, so that it cannot stick its fingers into the hole where its nose used to be.

Fanning its wings, it sails straight up into the air and, on still wings, drifts down again. And up and down again it sails, looking all over the sky for its nose; which is another proof that it does not think, for what, pray, would its nose be doing there? Until, by and by, it forgets all about the Nose of Gold, and forgets it is using its hands for oars. And then——

Well, of course, you know what it does at once. Just what you did with your tongue when you lost your tooth.

THE RELUCTANT MIRRORS!

WHY, I wonder, do grapes, certain berries, and some fruits, hide their purple faces within a dim veil of violet mists? Rose-coloured and purple plums, damsons, all dark grapes, and berries that are blue, retire behind veils of frosty shadows.

Is it that they, because of a strange, sweet reason, have taken the veil and live with their shining selves, like nuns, hidden in a silence of exquisite pain?

Perhaps, being so shiny, they were mistaken by the fairies for mirrors, which, when they were created, was not in the least intended, and fruits as they are, born of a royal purple lineage, resent certain winged creatures staring at their own likenesses, reflected in the fruits' shining rind. Maybe they did not understand their vanity, and thought

· "PERHAPS · BEING · SO · SHINY · THEY · WERE · MISTAKEN · BY ·
· THE · FAIRIES · FOR · MIRRORS" ·

that the fairies stood a little apart and glared at them with an excessive rudeness, for no reason at all.

And so, with a certain self-consciousness which comes in fruit that is born of a purple parentage, they remark with tilted noses: "I think we had better retire, my dears, behind the privacy of our veils!"

THE FANFARE

EYES have we with which to see; a nose for smelling; tongue for tasting; ears for hearing; and a heart we have with which to love. The fairies have as many senses as human beings have, and they have a few more, but they don't know it.

The fairies do not go to school as children do. They learn everything they have to know from their mothers, as bugs, and birds, and bunnies do, and as babies learn all the nicest things that they know from their mothers,—and the only things they can never forget.

The fairies have a sense that stays up in the little horns that grow out of their foreheads. All flying creatures have it growing somewhere. It keeps them from butting into anything, and they can fly anywhere they like, and do not have to look where they are flying. Human beings do not have this sense, for if they do not look where they are walking, they will stump their toes.

And the fairies possess a sense of play that human beings have when they are born into this world, but nearly always they lose it. If a fairy feels his play getting lost, he must lie on his back and each member of the tribe to which he belongs has one tickle at him, which is the very best medicine for this malady.

This, you must surely know, is catching.

If it cannot be tickled back into the place it belongs, the Apothecary, with his quill made of a feather from a starling's tail, and with the crimson juice of the pokeberry weed, writes a sign which is posted on the patient's chest.

It reads: "GROWING UP!"

When the dreaded words appear, it is a sign that he is to be exiled from his tribe. Silently a solemn ceremony is performed.

A petal from a flower is stuck on a stalk of

grass. The whole tribe march with a little droning sound to an open place in the weeds. He who is to be expelled holds the petal high and cries:

"Fanfare! Fanfare! Fanfare!"

and the wind blows the petal in the direction he must take.

Then everyone in the tribe trims one finger-nail in a fond farewell to the one who is leaving. In return he sticks out his tongue at each one of them, and flies off as the kindly wind has directed him, to find a new tribe.

This seems very sad, but it isn't. The fairies are everywhere, and a strange creature only has to answer one question to be admitted into a tribe, and that question is:

"Can you chew on both sides?"

GIVING THANKS

EVERYBODY and everything in this world wants a child of some sort of its own. There are some who are thankful for one child, others who are not contented when they have a hundred.

The oak tree, after a long time of wanting many children every year, has learned that there is not room for all the children it wants to be brought up in proper oak-tree fashion. Therefore, it spills, out of the little cups in which they sit, those acorns that grow straight up on the branches, thus giving a chipmunk a delightful dinner. The little cups, being empty, soon fill with a cool drink of drops of dew and rain.

Now, there are fairies who cannot abide frost, and migrate with their winged kindred, the birds, to warm southern lands. Nothing makes one so thirsty as long and high flights, and so the oak finds happiness in providing a refreshing drink for these birdlike beings as they stop in its branches to rest their wearied wings.

Therefore, for a dinner is the chipmunk thankful; for a refreshing drink to a thirsting throat is every migrating fairy thankful; and for little loving services to others is the oak tree thankful, which, after it has seen the joy in a fairy's face when the thirst is quenched, says in a soft rustling of russet leaves: "Oh, dear! Oh, dear! It is almost as sweet to be kind to another's child, as it is to be kind to a child of one's own!"

· "THE · OAK · FINDS · HAPPINESS · IN · PROVIDING ·A· REFRESHING ·
· DRINK · FOR · MIGRATING · FAIRIES" ·

FAIRY RING

(*Suggested by Jean Ingelow*)

THE tribe of fairies that are called the "One-foot ones" cannot abide the cold weather. And so, with the first descent of that obnoxious and destructive creature, Mr. Jonathan Frost, they bury themselves.

As the crimson leaves dance down the autumn breezes, they form themselves into little circles, and go up the grass in swerving circles, turning their toes in; and down the grass in even circles turning their toes out. And up, toeing out; and down, toeing in! Up, toeing out. Down, toeing in. Until one of them gives a call like a singing bird on a golden noon in springtime:

"Oh, speral, speral! Oh, holy, holy! Oh, clear away, clear away; clear up, clear up!"

And each digs a little hole.

The one who is first to finish his hole jumps in, and his next-door neighbour covers him up, and then jumps into his own hole and gets covered up in his turn.

Then around, and around, and around, until there is only one left. He flies off and joins another circle, hoping that he will have better fortune than to be the last the next time.

Once upon a time I asked a One-foot one: "Why do you do it?"

The fairies never have a reason for anything. They say, "Old Mother Fate makes us do it. For that that is, is; and when it is, it is as it is, that is the reason that it is." (Which, if one is a fairy, is a very good reason for such a delightful performance.)

And the next day, they sprout, and come up. They are not fairies at all, but those who were good children are *Mushrooms*, and those who were bad children are *Toadstools*.

SNAKEDOCTOR

ALACK-THE-DAY! Dear me! Whatever shall I do?

A fairy maiden has swooned in the shadow of a melon vine!

Ding-dong-dell! Ding-dong-dell!

Ring all the bells in your purple belfry, O Brother Columbine!

Send the tinkle ringing around, and around, all ye little flowers that bear as your bloom a bell, unto the time of its echoing through the daffy-down-dilly and thus awaken the dreaming dragon fly.

O pollen-powdered clappers, strike your flower bells, sending forth a resonance of sounds on every wave of sweet odour that arises from your silken throats!

Are you human folk aware that fairy ladies

fly forth in the evening in order that they may bathe in the sweet winds of twilight, and perchance have a dinner with those creatures that partake of a silken soft meal by starlight?

Twinkle tinkle! Tinkle twinkle!

Ring! oh, ring, Sweet Columbine!

A lovely lady has fallen in a swoon beneath the leaves of a melon vine.

Fairy ladies never faint save when they look into the blue eyes of a lover who has forsaken his loved one in May.

Therefore, O Snakedoctor, hasten with your leaf litter to a lady in sore distress.

Behold, at last, he comes and the pale green-winged stretcher bearers tenderly lift up the fairy maiden and lay her on their leaf.

"Ahem! Ahem!" says grave Doctor Dragon Fly. "A heaping eyeful of loveliness immediately."

Then he counts and counts her minute pulse.

"One, two, three, four, five, six, seven. Very weak! Very weak!

"O Little Elves of Loving Kindness, bear her on your swift, glad wings past the rarest aspect in·the garden.

"One, two, three, four, five, six, seven. Without another pulse beat I can effect no cure."

Over the gilly-flower and over the sweet rocket, they bear the dragon fly's fair patient, a-searching for her lost pulse beat.

"One, two, three, four, five, six, seven——"

Still seeking, they float with her through the aromatic odours arising from the bergamot and herb o'grace, and drift by the drooping heads of love-lies-a-bleeding.

Would you human folk care to know the Snakedoctor's balm for a fair lady who lies in a swoon?

His prescriptions are compounded solely for the eye and the ear.

℞   The Anodyne.
      It is Springtime! A cardinal bird woos his
mate on a wistaria vine.
    Sings he in his song to her:—
"Violet's blue, blue—Twinkle tinkle!
    Lavender's green, green.
When I am king, king—Tinkle twinkle!
    You shall be queen, queen."
While his mate dreams of a little bird in its shell.

What lost pulse could resist that?

"O dear Doctor! O dear Doctor!" softly hums
the fairy lady as she beholds his healing cure.

Twinkle tinkle! Tinkle twinkle! Thus did
the columbine swing on the wind of evening.
Will not you human folk admit that its swaying
brings such sweet results?

"One, two, three, four, five, six, seven,——"
O dear! O dear!— "EIGHT!"

Found is the little lost pulse beat. Therefore,
cured is the fainting fairy lady. Therefore,
proud is the learned dragon fly.

And as for you human folk, would you not do

· "AN · ANODYNE · FOR · SWOONING · FAIRY · LADIES · IS · TO · BE ·
CARRIED · PAST · CARDINAL · BIRDS · SINGING · ON · A ·
· WISTARIA · VINE" ·

well to take his nostrum? At least beware lest you increase too much his labours.

O lovers, leave not your mates in Maytime. And you who are lonely, return to your loved ones at once. If not in honour of Love and the Spring, then for the sake of fairy ladies who may, perchance, look into your eyes, and hence fall in a swoon within the cool shadow of a melon vine.

ZOOM, ZOOM!

ZOOM, Zoom! Zoom, Zoom!
It is time for all little crawling creatures
to go home and say, "God bless Mother and
Father, and make me a good little bug," and
jump into their beds.

Zoom, Zoom! Zoom, Zoom!

It is the time for the loveliest lady of all the
ladies who dwell in the land of the fairies, to
take her evening walk.

Fourteen fairy maidens, for fourteen moonlit
nights, ripped away the tissue of leaves to obtain
the veins of lacy net which forms her overskirt.
Others held the distaff and spun and wove her
train from stamens of moonflowers and evening
glory.

Of all the ladies who sojourn in the land of
fairies, she alone is indulged with the privilege

of wearing two maple seeds fastened to a ribbon that is bound around her wrist. Others, less favoured, are allowed only one.

Fairy ladies dare not lead little dogs on leashes between the avenues of weeds, lest all suddenly, they should have a fancy to fly up and soar over a blooming bush, in order that they may bathe in the odour thereof. In such a case, the little dog would hold them down to the earth. So, fairy ladies lead forth a moth, leashed on a thread of spider's silk, that their pets may float with them through perfumed paths.

This loveliest of all the fairy ladies is surrounded by a circle of blue musicians, each piper blowing the same note on his pipe:

Zoom, Zoom! Zoom, Zoom!

And thus in the hour of pastime, fairy ladies are thoughtful enough to perform little services for others. For, when these pipes sound, all the little crawling creatures know it is time to go, home.

Zoom, Zoom! Zoom, Zoom!

The little pageant is passing beneath the branches of a horse-chestnut tree, which is trying to bring up her children in a highly polished fashion. Five weeks longer of delicious sleep on the tree is allotted them before their shells pop and they fall down into the world to seek their fortunes.

And yet, what fortunes can be theirs except to be beautiful, as they lie in the grass?

Zoom, Zoom! Zoom, Zoom!

How could even the most well-behaved chestnut children sleep amid such noise? So they make faces at, and say dreadful words in horse-chestnut language to, the lady who is the unconscious disturber of their sleep.

One stops complaining long enough to look at his brothers. He laughs and laughs and laughs, until he loosens his stem!—and no wonder.

Now, had this tale been told you a second

later than the present moment, you might have
learned how he fell off the tree five weeks before his mother intended that he should.

WARFARE

(*The Mobilization of the Fairy Army*)

THE fairies do everything that human beings do, but cut their second teeth. This
they cannot do, because they do not shed their
first teeth.

Therefore, the fairies have measles, mumps,
and war.

Here you see the mobilization of the Fairy
Army. They have acorn helmets, and their
cruellest weapon is a grass-blade sword—one of
the blades of grass that grow up, bend over, and
wave back and forth on the gentlest wind of
June. These grass-blades, when blown on as
you hold them between the thumbs, thus, make
fine whistles.

The Major General of the Fairy Army does
not say, as Major Generals usually do: "Ready!

· " THE · MOBILIZATION · OF · THE · FAIRY · ARMY " ·

Aim! Fire!—Bang! Shoot everybody in sight!"

On the contrary, he says: "Thumbs up! Toes out! Fly softly to your enemy and, with your grass-blade sword, strike him very gently on the right cheek—smile sweetly; and strike him very gently on the left cheek, and smile sweetly. Then, in humble fashion, turning your toes in, fly back to your own camp in a glorious flight of victory!"

SAND

SWISH —swash; swish—swash.

Adorning themselves in white caps of innumerable bubbles, the waves break into the quiet of the sands.

Swish —swash; swish—swash.

In curling feathers of foam the waves roll into the sands' domain as far as they dare, and hastily withdraw.

Swish—swash; swish—swash.

With an endless lapping they mark their intrusion and departure by a wet amethyst trail that follows the shining reaches of the shore.

The fairies do not live for ever in the invisible land of fairies. They die after a period of exquisite existence of laughter, merriment, and mirth.

In the unsalted water of a lake, the tribe to

which he belongs buries the dead fellow creature
with a ceremony of exceeding sweetness. The
warm light of the sun and the cool moonlight
shining through the endless tossing of the waves,
here and there, purify the little beings, until
soon there remains, of what was once a fairy: a
shell, a frame, a grain of amber, amethyst, or
orange sand.

In the land in which fairies dwell, little loving
services to others are the greatest joys they know.
What else could their Paradise be save a place
wherein they create loveliness that human beings'
endless quest for beauty may be somewhat
satisfied?

After the purification by the warmth of the
sun, the cool light from the moon, and the washing of the waves, they assemble in vast hosts on
the shores of a lake, speck by speck, grain by
grain—amber, saffron, and silver—a million tiny
souls of fine, fine sand; wee particles of dust to
which they have returned.

Innumerable as the constellations, with hush, stillness, and peace, they sift like a silent tempest into little vales and plateaux, each hot dry plain bordered by faded-gold beach grass. The shadows of the stalks move back and forth. When the wandering wind, with its uneven winnowing, approaches a stalk of grass, the stem bends, and around and around in a silver furrow trails the mighty plume, bowed in a swoon to the earth by ardent wooing.

A stronger current of wind from another direction will soon obliterate the furrowed circle, cleaning the surface of the plain as a child with a sponge erases the long sums of division from its slate. It is thus prepared for new carving in high or low relief—the paired footprints of furred creatures, or the bold tracks of sea-birds.

And then the whole surface of the plateau is spoiled with swerving line upon line of undulating waves without foam. And yet the soundless billows mount so high that the crest of every wave is followed by a thin shadow of lavender. On all sides stretch wave upon wave of wind-blown sand that will give no ship a voyage save some bronze leaf that makes for no earthly port.

Flowing and trailing, the dust-souls of departed fairies pile themselves into miniature mountains where we may stand and behold the stars and the spaces between the stars. Every amber fairy-shell is willing to be submerged in immeasurable damp depths so that those who are fortunate enough to be sown on high may see the untold myriads of stars. In their eagerness to give to some one the gift of a sight of limitless pastures of beauty, impulsively shifting in a blinding flight, they cover flowers and bushes and trees. And thus their little shining selves shroud the forest they have stifled.

They withdraw themselves in trailing veils from the roots of trees and leave gaunt forms to be swept by the wind. With the changing sapphire lights, they pour a mountain of grains of sand as a grave-cloth over evergreen trees, leaving a valley that might have been moulded on the face of the moon.

In the springtime they crowd their hills and valleys with flowers that recall the departed hours of youth. With an inward glow that drenches the night, they trace some cousinship with the innumerable stars.

There is no sound save the lapping of the waves and the soughing of winds in the trees. The Dunes of Sand are the fairies' Paradise, where they are eternally happy, making endless beauty and creating a pavilion of silence into which we too can enter and find a sanctuary of sweet peace and rest.

STAY-AT-HOME HEART

STAY-AT-HOME HEART

THE castle of the King, who ruled over the Kingdom on the Silver Cliffs, crowned the highest peak of the white rocks that rose out of the blue, blue sea. On the top the cliffs were flat, and there the palace stood. It was built of white stones, with many turrets and innumerable windows. Very white and steep were the cliffs, at the foot of which the fishermen's houses were crowded together along the seashore. When the sun set, beyond the sea, every crystal window flamed with the reflection thereof. And out on the sea the fishermen, from their boats, could see the castle shining on the white rocks, like a silver crown on a gray-headed king.

On the fourteenth day of July the whole castle was aflutter with excitement. The christening of the Princess Clio Clementine Caroline

Cyclamen Candace Columbine was the most magnificent christening that had ever been known in the Kingdom on the Silver Cliffs.

All the bells in the castle rang out as the procession trailed over the carved yellow stones in the courtyard. Through the lilies and small pomegranates growing at intervals in large blue jars, the Grand Almoner scattered broadcast the choicest sweetmeats, while he led forth the train, with the heralds blowing upon their brass horns.

The Archbishop and the Privy Councillors came next, attended by the Prime Minister, courtiers, chancellors and the lords of the Court, the under-secretary and the clerks. The father and mother of the little Princess, the King and Queen, followed the clerks. The Junior page boys scattered wild flowers in the path before the Chief Cradle-rocker, who carried the little girl.

Six names were to be given the little Princess. She was clothed in the same christening robe of lace in which her mother, and her grandmother,

and her great-grandmother had once upon a
time been christened. Following the nurses to
the little Princess, in proper order, marched
the Princesses of the Court, Duchesses and
Marchionesses, Countesses and Viscountesses,
Baronesses, Maids of Honour, Ladies of the
Bedchamber, guards, grooms and lackeys, the
cooks and scullions.

When the grand procession had slowly passed
through the doorway of the chapel, the chimes
were silent. The King commanded every one
of his subjects, including the bell-ringers, to be
present at the great event.

When the christening ceremony was over the
Grand Almoner asked the people to follow him
into the garden of the castle. Suddenly the bells
began to peal forth again, and guns were fired to
announce the importance of the affair. Flags
waved everywhere on poles, as the crowd came
down the broad paths laughing, and singing, and
shouting, while the soldiers of the King came to

a halt and presented arms. All the people who were ruled by the King of the Silver Cliffs were wild with delight when they heard that their princess was now the possessor of six names.

"Long live the Princess! Long live our little Princess!" shouted the Marchionesses and the scullery maids.

A feast was spread under the horse-chestnut trees. And on the lawn, fountains poured forth streams of water, just for this especial day. Everyone was presented with a sweetmeat that was hidden within a heart-shaped paper. Each guest ate his sweetmeat as he received it, save one—an uninvited guest who had come and witnessed the christening, unnoticed. The light that shines in the young of heart was gleaming in her eyes. She moved forward, like a young girl, in her sea-green cloak. Around her waist was bound a girdle of rainbow-coloured ribbons.

You must now suspect, from what I told you of the way she looked, that she was a fairy. She was a fairy indeed. All this took place in the days when every good child had a fairy godmother—not so very long ago.

Now, if all godmothers are fairies, then one fairy still dwells in the world to-day. I know a boy who has a godmother.

This sister of the fairies did not eat the sweetmeat with the other guests. She hid it in a reticule that hung on a cord from her wrist. When she was sure that all the guests were engrossed in the feast of sugar-plums, nectarines, eitrons, and other delightful things that were now being passed amongst them by the pages, she withdrew from the crowds gathered around the tables, and went to have one look at the little princess that was permitted everyone present.

As she stood at the foot of the royal cradle, she spread her arms, like the wings of a bird on the point of flying.

"I am your Godmother," she said, scarcely above a whisper.

"I came uninvited to your christening. My sisters, the fairies, sent me here, to present to you three gifts.

"Their first gift to you is a name. By the fairies you will be called Cynthia, because, you shall be as beautiful as the crescent moon setting in a twilight of April.

"And the fairies give you a star, all for your own. The North Star is yours. You must watch for this star every cloudless night. If you never fail to bear loving kindness in your heart for my kinsfolk while you look at your star, when, someday, love comes into your life it will never, never leave you."

The little Princess Cynthia took her thumb out of her mouth. She lay very still, in her silken covers, as her godmother gave her the last gift.

"Listen well, Godchild, as I give you the third gift. You are granted the privilege of making one wish—only a single wish that will surely come true. Cherish the last gift. Save it until you are in need of fairy consolation."

This may seem strange to you, if you have tried to talk to a baby. But it is not. The fairies always talk to babies, that is, before babies learn to say human words. Babies learn all the strange, pretty things they do from the fairies. Sometimes they even say fairy words—strange little sounds, like crowing, that set the mother wondering what her child is trying to say.

After many years, the three gifts from the fairies were the only things Cynthia remembered of all that came to pass on the day she was christened.

The fairy godmother returned to the crowds that were now talking and laughing in gay groups in the garden. After she had eaten one nectarine, she moved quietly to the great gates of the castle. Then she slipped away, without any one, save the Princess Cynthia, having noticed that she was among the guests. But the

Princess said "ta ta," and other fairy words, as she again slipped her pink thumb into her mouth.

The fairy godmother hurried away from the festivities, which lasted until after the sun had set. She had promised the fairies to be present at another christening. It was to take place in a fisherman's cottage that stood in the fishing village, tucked away among the rocks, at the foot of the Silver Cliffs. No one witnessed this event, save the mother and father of the boy with eyes as blue as the gentians that grew beside the stream in the forest up on the cliffs. There was no feast or celebration as this boy was named David, after his father, his grandfather, and his great-grandfather, who had, in their turn, been fishermen to the kings that had ruled over the Kingdom on the Cliffs.

When the fairy godmother had given three gifts to the fisherman's son, she retired to the land of the fairies. There she was very happy and lived for a long time.

Now, if you are a friend of the fairies, you may call this little girl Cynthia, as I am privileged to do. But, if for any reason, you are not on good terms with the fairy-folk, you must call her all six names, given to her by the Archbishop at her christening, Clio Clementine Caroline Cyclamen Candace Columbine.

The Princess Cynthia grew up, as little princesses are wont to do. Still she played with her golden ball, in the King's garden, by the pool that splashed incessantly as the water from the fountain fell into it.

Down on the white sands of the beach, David grew strong and fair and brave. Just as it should be, he became a fisherman, as his father and his grandfather had been good fishermen in their day. Every morning, David went out upon the sea, in one of the fishing boats, with his father and the other fishermen. At the hour when the reflection of the setting sun shone in the castle windows, they returned with the boats filled with shining fish. When the fishermen caught a fine fish, they brought it to the kitchen door of the castle and gave it to the cook.

Every evening, when the sky was clear, the Princess Cynthia looked far over the sea and up to her star. Then she would send a message of love to her fairy godmother. And down on the sea, David looked up at the shining turrets of the castle, from the boats, as they returned to the shore.

Cynthia had scarcely reached the age of sixteen when many kings sought her hand for the young princes of the neighbouring kingdoms. One day, her father, having perceived the wealth of some of the kings, called his daughter to him.

"My dear child," he said, "the time is approaching when you must give up playing, and prepare to be a queen. You shall have a husband and I a son-in-law. I am wiser than you are, therefore I shall choose a husband for you. Play on with your golden ball. When I have found the proper prince for your heart and hand, I will call you from your play."

Before the King could choose among the many suitors, a strange prince arrived. He came from a kingdom twelve thousand leagues away. He was so rich and powerful that the King could not resist listening to his address.

The sun was shining on the pool in the King's garden, making the water of the fountain glisten like stars as it leaped into the air. The little Princess rolled her golden ball from the shadow of the mimosa tree into the sunshine. Her golden hair gleamed like the primroses that grew in a circle around the fountain. She was far too happy in her play to lose one moment of it. Therefore she sent one of her maids to peep through a break in the syringa hedge. There the little maid was to see the visiting prince. Then, when Cynthia grew tired playing with her ball, she could hear how the man looked to whom she was to give her heart and her hand.

Especially, did she bid the maid listen to the words the Prince said to her father.

The maid stood on tiptoes and looked through the branches of the hedge. She saw a large coach, shining in the sunlight. The wheels were gilded and the cushions were red, with many tassels that waved on the wind. It was drawn by eight horses as white as snow. The harness and reins were of red leather. The steeds started impatiently and their hoofs stamped the flagstones. A number of footmen in red coats, armed and mounted on white horses, were grouped around the coach.

The maid listened, but the horses and footmen made such a noise that she could hear nothing the rich Prince said to the King, save that he did not have a mother.

When she returned to the pool, the Princess Cynthia had forgotten the errand on which she had sent her maid. Therefore, they tossed the golden ball into the air, until the sun moved

behind the castle turrets, and the garden turned
cool in the shadow. A page brought tea to the
Princess in the garden. The visiting prince
drove away amid a clatter of hoofs and wheels.
This reminded the Princess that she had not
asked the maid what manner of man this was to
whom she was commanded to give her heart.
She asked the question with her mouth full of
cooky and jam.

"He is old and fat with a long red beard,"
replied the maid.

"Ugh! And what did he say?"

"'My father is the King of the Sunken
Meadow; I have no mother,'" quoted the maid,
affecting haughtiness.

"I will not give him my heart and my hand,"
Cynthia said, as she left the table and cast her
ball into the air. It fell with a splash into the
water of the pool and was lost amongst the long
swaying stems of the water-lily pads.

After the King had eaten his supper, he sent

for the Princess Cynthia. He told her he had chosen a fine and proper husband for her.

"He is the Prince of the Sunken Meadow. He is very rich and in a little while will be a king. Then you will be a queen."

"I do not want to be a queen. I would rather just be happy. Nothing will induce me to marry this prince, father. I do not want to go twelve thousand leagues away. I want to stay at home, beside my own blue sea."

Cynthia was determined, and poked out her lower lip, which, in Cynthia, expressed stubbornness.

"Hoity-toity!" said the King. This he never said but when he was provoked. "Why not? —pray tell me."

"I have heard that he has three wrinkles across the back of his neck; the prince to whom I give my hand shall not have one wrinkle. He has a beard, a long red beard; the prince to whom I give my heart must love butter, or else I could not endure him. Now, how on earth can a buttercup prove that any one loves butter, if a long red beard covers up his chin?

"Worst of all, he admitted that he had no mother. I will not marry a man who has no mother!"

And she took refuge in the arms of her own mother with such pitiful and tender trust that no one but a king who has gout could have had such a hard heart.

"Hoity-toity!" said the King again, which was a very bad sign. He withdrew from the room, limping on a crutched stick.

He ordered the First Lord of the Court to shut up his daughter in a high turret in a remote corner of the castle, where she could speak to no person for eight days. Cynthia pleaded with her father. But all her entreaties were to no purpose. Everyone in the kingdom must obey the King. He then ceased to think on the subject. The little Princess, seeing what her father had done, fell

down in a swoon, and a guard carried her tenderly up the winding stairway.

Eight days the Princess Cynthia sat among
her cushions, in a room in the turret with the
long circling stairs, winding her distaff. But
often she had to untangle the matted thread.
Eight evenings, as the fishermen's boats returned
homeward over the sea, she looked out of the large
round window, waiting for the sun to set. When
the light faded from the sky, the steadfast star would
shine down on her. It was her only consolation.

She watched the line of boats draw near the
beach. The fishermen looked up from the sea
at the weather-cock on the castle turret, swinging to and fro on the wind of the evening, and
the sunlight, shining on the glass in the windows, dazzled their eyes. The golden ball was
lost in the pool in the King's garden. In the
wistaria vines, that trailed from the foot of the
cliffs up to the window in the castle turret, the
ring-doves cooed their saddest twilight notes.

"Surely, of all the people who live in my father's kingdom," thought the little imprisoned Princess, "there is none so lonely and sad of heart as I am."

The light faded in the sky. She felt that her heart must surely break.

"How long am I to be held a captive in my father's prison?" she sighed.

Over the sea the stars began to twinkle. As she blew a kiss out of the window, for the fairies, she sent a message of love and belief in them.

The silence of the night was broken by a ringing knock on the door, followed by the entrance of the King and Queen. Two men stepped inside the room with flaming torches.

"Are you ready for your wedding to the Prince of the Sunken Meadow?" asked her father, the ruler of all the people who lived in his kingdom.

"I am not ready, Father, because there will
not be any wedding to that Prince," she mildly
replied.

"We will see!" roared the king, "we will see!"

He hit the floor with his stick, calling to the
Queen to follow him at once.

"On the fourteenth day from to-day you will
marry whomsoever I wish. I am the ruler of
this house and I see that my subjects obey!"

The Queen took Cynthia in her arms and
kissed her many times. Cynthia laid her head
on her mother's shoulder. Surely this place
would not fail her now.

"My poor little child," wept the mother with
her heart full of pain. "I am your mother, but
I am powerless to save you from this great hurt.
I, who love you better than anything in the
world, must submit to your father's cruelty."

"Come at once, wife!" angrily shouted the
King from without the door.

The Queen laid a bunch of wild flowers on

Cynthia's lap. She left her child alone in the dark tower.

The knocking of the King's stick on the steps faded away down the stairway. Fainter and fainter grew the sound of the footsteps of these two whose love for each other had ceased to give any light in their lives a few years after the birth of their daughter.

Left in the darkness, Cynthia wiped the tears from her eyes. She looked out upon the sea and then up to the stars that were now shining above the dark water. Very sorrowful she was and sad and sweet, like a pansy hidden among many leaves, as she sat in the midst of the cushions.

Again Cynthia was beginning to cry, when suddenly she remembered her fairy godmother. What godmother ignores the need of a child, especially when that child has been deserted by those who should cherish her? Therefore, she thought, would there be any other time in her

whole life when she would need, more than at
this time, the fulfilling of the wish the fairies
had granted her on the day she was christened.
Surely no greater ill-fortune could befall her.
She was a prisoner in her father's house, with
her only hope of liberty the marriage to a man
who did not have a mother.

Thus she sat all through the night, unable to
determine whether or not this was the proper time
to ask her one assured wish of the fairies.   But
how could she be sure of wishing wisely? She was
still so young. All the days of her life had
passed so quickly by. She had only played
carelessly with her golden ball. What else did
she know to make her happy, but to go on
playing with her golden ball? She did not
know what to ask of the fairies, that would save
her from the cruel plan her father seemed determined to carry out.

The stars faded one by one as the gray light
of dawn spread over the sky. When the first

ray of the rising sun threw a gold beam upon
the sea the fishermen rowed their boats out and
cast the nets into the water.

Worn and tired, after the long, sleepless night,
Cynthia was still unable to determine what
would save her from this plight. Not knowing
why she did so, she arose and walked very
slowly to the window. With the same faith in
her heart that had made her find the North
Star in the sky every night, she raised her hands
as if in prayer. She asked her godmother,
wherever she might be, in some way to come to
her or to send a message that would tell her what
it was she must now ask of the fairies.

"O Godmother, send me a low sweet nest,
Wherein my breaking heart may rest."

She said this out loud. Thus did she make
the one wish that would surely come true. But
she did not know it.

After Cynthia had given the wish to the wind,
to be borne away on its invisible wings to her

godmother, she said these same words over and over again. But she did not know why she repeated them so often.

When the sun was well up in the sky, from afar over the blue sea there flew a great sea-green bird. The sunlight flashed on its spread wings, as it moved up and down with the tossing of the waves, coming nearer and nearer to the shore. Around and around the turrets of the Castle of the Silver Cliffs it flew, calling to the wild gulls that were nesting in the crevices of the rocky cliffs. Around and around the turret that held prisoner a little princess, it wheeled, sending a great call echoing across the sea.

Cynthia, upon hearing the bird's strange cry outside the turret window, flung open the casement. The bird alighted on the window ledge. It flapped its wings with a great noise and then folded them. Then it preened the feathers of its rainbow breast.

Cynthia stirred like a wild flower on a gentle wind, and said:

> "O sea-green bird with rainbow breast,
> Sing me a song of a low sweet nest,
> Wherein my breaking heart may rest."

Now, if you have a fairy godmother, you, too, might have heard the song the sea-green bird with the rainbow breast and gold tail-feathers sang to the unhappy Princess. But if you are one of those who have no fairy godmother and have never heard such a song, I will tell you, as well as I am able, how the song sounded.

"*O Speral, Se-u-re!* The water in the pool in the King's garden is never, never still It is stirred incessantly by the fountain, that rises in a slim column and then falls among the lilies that grow therein. By the rim of stones that encircle the pool in the King's garden two yellow irises arise out of the damp earth and lift up their heads to the sun. The two irises cannot see one another face to face over the water. Between them a woodbine vine trails its leaves and tendrils in the small waves that lap the smooth stones below with a gentle sound. But they can see one another's distorted image, as they sway back and forth, reflected in the moving water. *O Speral, Se-u-re!*"

The song being sung, again the bird preened the feathers of its rainbow breast. A blue feather caught in its beak and clung there for a moment. Then it drifted down to the Princess's feet. The bird spread its wings and took flight.

It flew in a straight line above the sea, and passed over the fishing boats, as they were tossed up and down with the waves. A fisherman shaded his eyes with his hand to look at it, and called to another fisherman, in a near-by boat:

"I have never seen a bird like that one in these parts before."

On and on the bird flew, until from the castle window Cynthia could only see a small gray spot against the sky. Its wings dropped lower and lower, until at last it sank so low that the foam of the waves dashed against its breast. Suddenly it dropped down into the sea. All of the bird save the rainbow-coloured feathers of its breast and one of the gold feathers from its tail dissolved and became part of the great blue ocean.

Those feathers of the great singing bird, that

· "THE · SEA · GREEN · BIRD · SANK · SO · LOW · THAT · THE · FOAM ·
· OF · THE · WAVES · DASHED · AGAINST · ITS · BREAST" ·

did not become a part of the sea, drifted to the
north and to the south, then to the east and to
the west, to be washed ashore later, on the beach
at the foot of the cliffs, when the sand was like
silver in the moonlight.

Meanwhile, back in her turret, Cynthia was
pondering over the song of the bird. Surely it
was a message from the fairies, in answer to her
plea to her Godmother.

"Two yellow irises, that can only see one
another's distorted image, as they sway back and
forth, reflected in the water of the pool in the
King's garden," repeated the imprisoned Princess to herself.

She looked out of the window and over the
sea, wondering what these words might mean.

Down on the sea the fishermen were returning homeward. David and the other fishermen
brought in their boats laden with fish. After
they had landed on the beach, far below the
window from which the Princess Cynthia looked

down on them, David brought the finest fish to
the kitchen door of the castle, and gave them to
the head cook.

As David, returning from the castle, reached
the beach, the wind of the twilight had begun
to blow and the moon was high over the sea,
throwing a silver quivering reflection, like a
path—on and on—farther out than David had
ever been in the fishing boats. He turned from
the temptation to follow in a quest of the moon-
silvered path, and started toward the cottage
where his mother was preparing the supper.

He had only taken a few steps homeward
when he paused, then returned and stood in the
first steps of the shining path in the water, where
the waves were breaking into pearls of silver
foam. As the cool water washed against his feet,
a cluster of brightly coloured feathers was borne
inward by the waves, and left on the wet sand.

All the world around him was an enchanted
place of moonlight and silver sand. The line of

curling foam stretched far to the north and to the south.

He took up the rainbow feathers. Then he twined around his body a long strand of a green weed that had grown in the depths of the sea. With this he bound the feathers against his bare chest as they had grown on the breast of the bird. The one gold tail-feather that had not dissolved with all the rest of the bird in the sea, he fastened to his forehead with another strand of sea-weed, so that the tip of the feather pointed to the Star of the North, now shining steadily over his head. And the quill pointed to his own heart.

Immediately David felt himself afire with wonder. And as if someone were leading him, he turned away from the path—homeward.

With lips parted and eyes afire, he marched, as though it were to the beating of the waves of the sea. Retracing the footpath over which he had recently come from the castle, down the moon-silvered beach he moved as one who walks in his sleep.

He came to the foot of the steep rocks, which rose abruptly from the sea and were crowned by the castle of the King. Two of the castle walls rose up here, as if they were a part of the cliff. A wistaria vine with a twisted trunk hung in a heavy mass from the castle walls as far up as the turret. Without knowing why, he made his way through the thick mass of leaves.

As he climbed higher and higher through the trembling vines, a shower of blooms fell to the ground below. The vines led him on and on until he came to the round window in the turret that looked out over the sea. He stepped onto the window-ledge, where he stood for a moment and looked past the great circle of moonlight that spread on the floor to the little Princess. She lay sleeping amongst her many coloured cushions. He looked on Cynthia with great tenderness and admiration.

An unknown magical power had brought him here. It was holding him immovable, spellbound, in the circle of moonlight. He did not know whether he ought to awaken her or leave her sleeping. Therefore, he stood pondering, filled with amazement at her great beauty. He saw tears falling from under her closed eyelids, and dropping from her cheek.

While David was thus engaged in thinking over what he should do, she awoke, and sat gazing at him with the lovely wondering eyes of a little child. He stood, tall and handsome, before her. His black hair was clinging in close curls to his sun-burned brow, and his eyes of blue were filled with the deepest tenderness.

As she looked at him, he kneeled in the moonlight beside her, and bowed his head almost to the floor. Cynthia was surprised, and a little frightened, at the appearance of this strange youth. She thought that he might be the Prince to whom she was expected to give her heart and her hand; and yet the little maid had said that *he* had a red beard.

"Stand up and turn all the way around," she commanded almost severely.

He stood for a moment looking at her and then turned slowly around. There was no sign of a red beard, or of *any* coloured beard. And there was not one wrinkle across the back of his neck.

"Did my father send you here to take my heart and hand?" Cynthia asked, greatly perplexed.

He shook his head slowly, as he said, "No." She could scarcely hear him.

"Are you one of the King's servants?" inquired the puzzled Princess.

"No," he answered fervently; "but since I came into this room, I am a servant in the court where you are the queen."

"I am not a queen yet," said the Princess in great surprise.

"You are the queen that has ruled over all my dreams," he said convincingly.

"What is your name?"

"David."

"How did you come here?"

"I have a Godmother, by whose magic, I am sure, I have been led here to lay my heart at your feet."

Although the Princess had been frightened, she noticed the softness of his voice and did not hesitate to look into his eyes. And then she saw the feathers like unto the bird that had sung of the two yellow irises.

"I do not see what it means," she said. And a silence fell between them.

"What is your name?" he asked at length.

"Clio Clementine Caroline Cyclamen Candace Columbine." She told him her name in a sing-song fashion. She could not say it otherwise.

"In the kingdom of my dreams, I have called you Cynthia."

"Cynthia!" The Princess looked startled. She had heard that name but once before.

"David, my friend," she said sweetly—"for a friend of mine I think you must be—I am very unhappy. And this is all so strange to me. I cannot tell whether I am awake or in a dream."

"Indeed, your friend I am," he answered eagerly. "You are not sleeping. But you are dreaming, and in this dream you shall have whatever you wish as soon as you tell me what it is." For David, too, had been given a wish by his godmother. And what more could he wish than that which she wished?

"My father is trying to make me marry a prince who has a red beard, but who has no mother."

He hesitated and then smiled with joy as he said: "If that is all that troubles you, I can easily put an end to your sorrow."

"How, pray tell me, would you do it?"

"Lay your head on my shoulder and believe all that it will say to you."

She pressed her cheek against the rainbow-coloured feathers of the singing bird on his breast. He kissed her hair.

"With your head resting there, can you doubt that I love you with all my heart?" he entreated.

"Only wait a little while and I believe I, too, will love you dearly."

Then Cynthia suddenly recollected the test which she had told her father must be passed by the man who was to win her hand and her heart. She reached over to the jar wherein the flowers that her mother had brought her were still fresh. Taking a buttercup from among the blooms, she held it under his chin. When she saw a pale yellow light reflected on his skin from the flower, she looked into his eyes and asked earnestly:

"Have you a mother?"

"Yes."

After a moment, wherein a thousand stars began to shine in dark places in the sky, she laid her cheek against the feathers on his breast. She murmured:

"My heart has found its low sweet nest, wherein it may have rest. O my dear, my dear; will it rest here always?"

And then she drew her head up, as a bird does when drinking. She looked into his eyes.

"For ever and ever and ever," he replied; "through the long nights and pale noons, and past the countless stars; when the city is whispering below us, or the water of the sea is lapping against the side of a boat; when we are in the light of the late coming moon of the South, or listening to the rustle of the understanding leaves. Always, within my heart will you rest."

There was no other sound save the waves washing up on the smooth sands of the beach

far below them; for the fountain in the King's
garden had ceased to leap into the air, and the
water in the pool thereof was still.

David tenderly carried the Princess Cynthia
down the steep descent, through the branches
of the wistaria vine, as though she were a little
child; he was taking her away from a prison to
a place amongst kind-hearted people, where she
would find rest for her heart and ease for the
sorrow of which her father had been the cause.
Their journey was as wonderful to them as
passing through the low clouds and showers of
spring, as sailing into the yellow sunset, as meeting the stars, and as roaming through a rainbow
in their happiness. They reached the beach at
the foot of the cliff. Hand in hand together
they went, in the moonlight, over the sand.

David, the fisherman's son, led the Princess
Cynthia to his mother, in her cottage by the sea.
She was a very wise woman, as mothers usually

are. At once she took Cynthia into her arms as though she were her own little child who had been lost but was found and returned to her after long, long waiting.

In the morning of the next day the marriage was celebrated. And the Princess Cynthia became a fisherman's wife. She was as happy as a princess or a fisherman's wife could be.

When the room in the castle turret was discovered empty, and the King's daughter was nowhere to be found, great were the regrets and the sorrow, loud the crying in the court. What could the King think, save that his harshness had forced the little Princess to throw herself from the turret window down into the sea? She had gone out of the hearts of those who should have cherished her for youth's sake, if for no other reason.

For Cynthia and David six years passed quickly by, as they always do when people are happy, and they are always happy when they stay near at home and do not quarrel. Long days of regret had softened the heart of the King, and the Queen grew more sorrowful as the years passed.

One day, when the sunshine was flooding the garden of the Castle on the Silver Cliffs, where the King and Queen were sitting under the spreading branches of the horse-chestnut trees, David and Cynthia brought a little boy to the castle. The King and Queen received them with forgiveness and great rejoicing. And it all ended just as it should end, when the King realized that, being a father, he could become a grandfather. And now he was invited to be a godfather.

What man—be he a king who rules over a kingdom, or fisherman who sails on the sea in his boat—could continue to be cruel-hearted when he is the father of a lost child who has returned, and the grandfather and the godfather of a little boy, at one and the same time?

While the Queen wept tears of thankfulness, the King had to take off his crown and smooth the dent it had made in his forehead. Replacing the crown on his own head, the King carried Cynthia's child into the chapel for the christening. After that, they went into the castle and the feast lasted into the night.

And the little boy became the ruler over the hearts of all those who sojourned within the Kingdom on the Silver Cliffs.

PORTRAITS

THE COMET'S TAIL

"THEY called it a tail! They called it a tail!"

The Comet King dashed across the sky faster than the fastest rocket.

"They called it a tail!" he screamed. He plunged into the cosmic seas where he butted into a star, breaking it into a million meteorites. These scattered out of his path, and, whirling themselves away, made courses in a strange orbit.

Now! For fourteen thousand years the Comet King had sat upon a cloud, combing his beard with a fine-tooth comb that was made of the rays of the setting sun and the light of the rising moon.

Seven times a day he anointed his beard with sunbeams and the dust of space. At night he burnished it with ashes of the bronze circle that oftentimes glows around the moon. In the spring the trailing flame-like beard that grew around his mouth was polished with star-beams. In the autumn it was sprinkled with the dust of drifting dreams.

At last, after years of solicitude, it was finer than the down on the breast of young birds.

On the day that followed after the anniversary of the fourteen thousandth year that this monarch had sat cross-legged upon a cloud, the fourth toe on the left foot went to sleep. Toes are wont to do so when they are not exercised. He remembered, as he stretched himself, once having heard that "sleeping toes can be awakened if one walks up and down." Indeed it would be pleasant to stroll amongst the constellations, and a pleasure to exchange a "How-do-you-do?" with his cosmic cousins, the orbéd spheres. Therefore, he roamed down an alley of space. Not once did this royal wanderer trip over his beard as it flowed behind his heels in league upon league of curling spray.

Behold! Certain planet ladies giggled. Tilting their noses coquettishly, they endeavoured to attract the attention of his haughty majesty by a subterfuge.

"What a beautiful tail!"

A *tail* indeed! As he heard this the hair on his head stood on end in a stormy hurricane. He did not stop to think; comets never do.

Gnashing his teeth and clenching his fist he folded his feet for a flight. Sparks flew from him and fluttered down the dark where they were quenched in the light of an oncoming dawn. Insulted to the innermost depths of his blazing being, he screamed forth a scroll of sparkling sound.

"They called it a tail! They called it a tail!"

He swept across the sky faster than the swiftest swallow. The hair on his head impaled stars, carrying them to places wherein they were overshadowed by greater stars and lost the song of their twinkling in a shining light.

He smashed others to pieces. The broken bits roamed blindly around and around until they found a course whereon they could swing and renew their silent singing. And still other stars were entangled in his beard and carried to remote places.

He plunged through clouds, tearing them into shreds. Hazy fragments clung to his breast and dimmed its shining. The silver linings of the clouds wound around his body and flashed as he rushed past the orb of the day.

His flight rent the rainbow into rags. A tangled streamer of indigo and orange fluttered behind him into unknown star-depths.

While passing the Pleiades there was no time for him to enquire whether or not they had found the little sister, lost to them ages and ages ago. So terrific was his speed, so violent was his exertion, that boiling sweat spangled the stars and planets about him. He passed through the bowl of the Great Dipper so quickly that not a drop of its luminary contents was spilled.

With dazzling explosions the Comet King left a blazing wake through the Milky Way, tearing a large enough rent in its closely studded bridge to attract the attention of the astronomers who dwell on Mercury, Mars, and Venus: That is, of such astronomers as *do* dwell thereon.

In utter rage the flying monarch bit a chip from the outer band of Saturn. But that did not make any difference to this planetary dealer in rings. Before one could say "Jupiter Robinson" Saturn had set the empty space with new moons.

The monarch absent-mindedly swallowed what was nothing less than a mouthful of moons— moons that wax and wane as moons are wont to do, and could not cease that regular performance even though they were swallowed by a Comet King.

He paused in his wild flight.

What other creature—be he comet, bird, or

machine—ever had to keep his mind on flying while moons waned within himself? It could not be done.

And so, the unreasonable king sipped a cool shower that was falling from some near-by clouds. The drops of the April rain were warm and dissolved the mass of moons from Saturn's bands within him.

This was the end of the comet's flight.

Swinging in remote space he remembered what had brought him here.

After all, he reflected, the planet ladies had merely *called* it a tail. Surely that did not *make* it one. However, for reassurance, he looked to see.

It was *not* a tail!

I-n-d-e-e-d! It—was—not—a—tail!

It was a shining beard that floated behind him for a million miles. It was only his own impatience of criticism that had made him a victim of their silly gossip and caused such needless destruction in the starry environs.

· "CALLING · IT · A · TAIL · DID · NOT · MAKE · IT · ONE" ·

He walked calmly back to the meadow of the meteors. Forgiving the planet ladies, he kissed them on the top of their heads where the rays start.

Finding a cloud whereon he could rest, he crossed his legs with dignity and sat himself down in the same position that had made his toe go to sleep and so created the turmoil.

He was fourteen thousand years untangling his beard and as he untangled, he pondered over his toes, speeding the ages away with a delightful riddle.

"Eni-Meni-Mini-Mo. Which one of my ten toes on which one of my two feet will be the next toe to take a nap?"

THE DAUGHTER OF A COMET KING

EVERYBODY and everything has a child of some sort of its own. Sometimes it is a baby, sometimes an acorn, and sometimes a little twinkling star.

Yes, stars have children and comets have children. Here is the picture of the Daughter of a Comet King.

The daughters of comets are not like their fathers, who dash across the sky faster than the fastest swallow and don't care a whit into what they butt, or into what small pieces they break it. They only stop long enough to laugh at the broken pieces and never say, "Excuse me!" as everyone really should.

Comet ladies just drift dreamingly about the sky, sweetly shunning every star and cloud,

"COMET · LADIES · DRIFT · DREAMINGLY · ABOUT · THE · SKY"

waving their arms this way and that way, sending soft flower-scented winds into our windows, and making the leaf-laden trees whisper: "Ah me, ah me! how sweet, how sweet, how sweet is the cool of the evening!"

THE GODMOTHER

TO-DAY all the world is to me as though it were a vast gray sea, and all the people on the world like ships.

Vessels—brigs and schooners, sloops and lighters—are passing back and forth through the sun-capped waves of days, and the nights that are the shadows of these endless billows.

There is a galley with a high prow putting into a port, and a noble three-decker with seventy guns proudly sets sail from her harbour. A frigate runs through a tempest and an ancient open barge with blue sails is drifting through sunlit waters. There are pirate ships plunging through the choppy seas of a gale after treasure. A fine bark is adrift in a field of icebergs, while a transport is lost in the fog. A merchantman is becalmed in a quiet sea and there are boats with sails set, but alas! they cannot sail, because there is no wind. Some of the vessels are bedecked with flags and pennons, while others follow great carved figureheads. Countless as the sands on the edge of the ocean are the crafts where their propellers mark their heart throbs.

Journeying through the seas of this life, every vessel needs must leave a wake of some sort behind it, as it moves through calm or troubled water. There are ships that leave trails of bubbles as clear as the dewdrops of spring. And there are others whose wakes are cloudy bubbles. Alas, Alas! Some boats are tracing their courses with paths of slime and dirt and destruction.

I am a craft, sea-worn and lonely. It is needful that I tow an excursion through the waves for the pleasure of my shipwright.

To-day as I sailed across a bay for a harbour wherein they tell me I may dream my dreams, I sighted a noble white vessel with silver sails

that curled in the wind like flower petals. I
gave her the right of way. The mighty argosy
passed before me. but I could not see the name
traced on the prow. I knew from the nobility
of the figurehead, whose eyes looked unflinch-
ingly into the face of the sun, that it was a
wondrous boat indeed.   .

O great white ship, with your silver sails, did
you dream of a little gray craft whose path you
crossed?

I sailed through your shining trail in the waves
of days and nights. Against my side I felt a
gentle clinking; leaning over my helm I looked
down into the water.

Behold! In the wake you are leaving behind
you, O shining white ship with your curling
sails, the bubbles have changed into pearls!

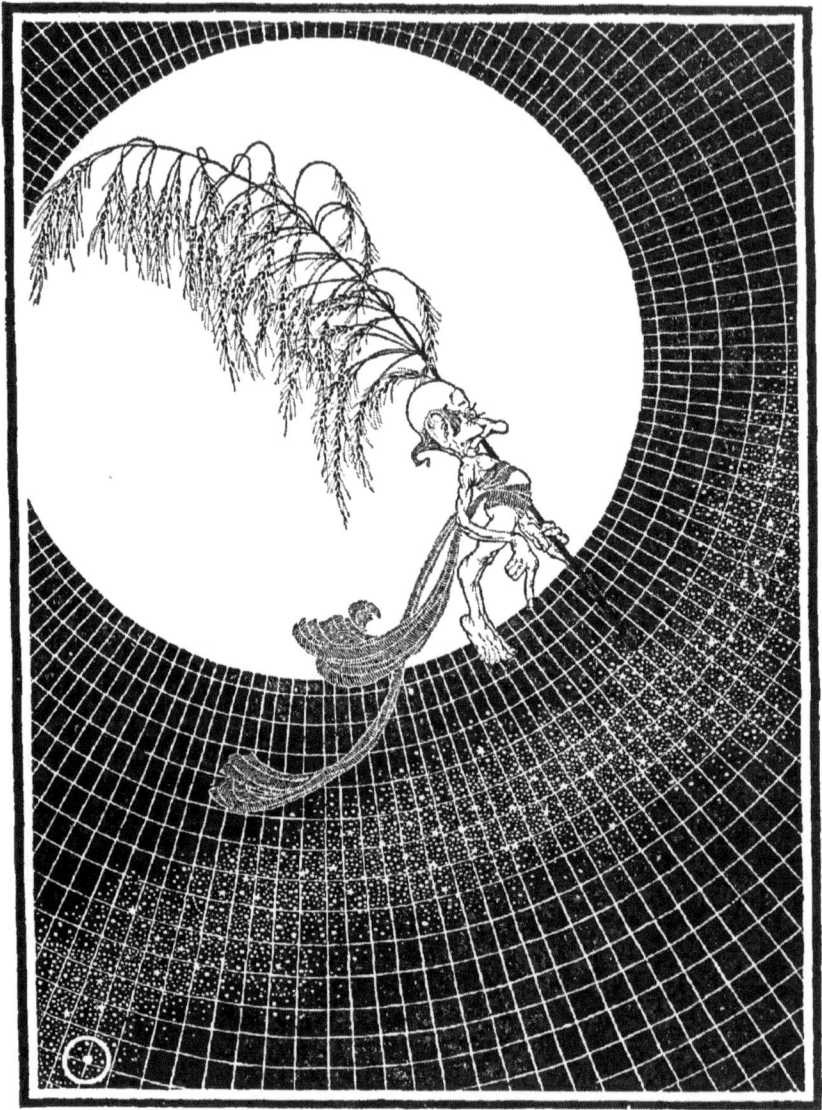

· " ONE · OF · THE · COMMON · DECENCIES · OF · ORDINARY ·
· SOCIAL · INTERCOURSE " ·

"ONE OF THE COMMON DECENCIES OF ORDINARY SOCIAL INTERCOURSE"

ON A day once upon a time when love should have been in every heart in the whole wide world, a man and a boy had a quarrel. What it was all about I am sure I do not know, and I do not think that they themselves know. Quarrels sometimes are that way.

However, I do know (and I will tell you) how it ended. The man made a face at the boy. His nose quivered three times (not being the quarreling man, or a rabbit, I cannot show you how) as he said:

"I shall no longer expect of you the common decencies of ordinary social intercourse."

The boy laughed and the quarrel was over.

Here you see a portrait of *one* of the common

decencies, those delightful etiquette creatures such as: "Keep-your-elbows-off-the-table"; "Speak-only-when-your-mouth-is-empty"; "Always-chew-with-closed-lips," and all that one should do. But how one ever does them all without going through life with a book of etiquette in his hip pocket, no one (except the person who does them all as they should be done) will ever know. The young gentleman who posed for this portrait is called: "Mr. Children-should-be-seldom-seen-and-never-heard."

THE MAGIC DEWDROP

THE MAGIC DEWDROP

ABOULHASSUM, Caliph of Iblis, possessed the most beautiful wife in all the lands of Saum, Mosul, and Ind, but had no children. This was a great grief to the Caliph and his subjects, especially when they remembered that, at his death, there would be no son to bear his name, and no heir to inherit his goods and lands.

At length, after years of unhappiness, he could bear it no longer and sent his faithful Vizier to a mighty magician to beg him to cast some spell by which the great calamity which was falling on his house might be averted.

Mirtas of the silver hair, mightiest magician in all the land, came into the presence of the Queen and said: "O great and beautiful Queen, your wish is about to be fulfilled. I pray you, go into the garden of the lilies, when the flowers are silvered by the moon and are lulled to dreams by the doves cooing their melancholy tale of love. There you will find a lily whose face looks up to the heavens. Therein will be a dewdrop that holds in its surface the image of a reflected star. When the throats of the singing sunbirds that nest among the lilies, are fresh with the cool of dawn, drink this dewdrop, and think of the stars."

The beautiful Queen did all that Mirtas of the silver hair told her to do.

On a night when the doves cooed as though their hearts would break and the moon was on the wane, a child was born to the wife of Aboulhassum, Caliph of Iblis. It was a boy and there was a hump on his back. His mother called him Selim (a Guiding Star); and for one short hour she loved him beyond everything in the world, and died.

There was a hump on little Selim's back and as he grew older, it bowed his head to the earth, so that when he sat and dreamed of what his life might have been, his chin rested on his knee. But in his eyes was the beauty of the image of a setting star reflected in the pale cool water at dawn.

There are many among us who see the reflection of a star, and yet whose eyes pass over its beauty to seek what is held in the deep water beyond the reflection, and few among us who see its beauty and let their eyes linger on its quivering image until the star has set. So there were few, in the days of Aboulhassum, who saw the beauty of Selim's eyes, and many who did not, for their eyes ever passed beyond his face and rested upon the hump on his back. His body grew so ugly and illshaped that not one of the attendants would speak to him, and he never failed to excite laughter and ridicule among those who should have cherished him, if for no other reason than for the sake of his beautiful mother, who had loved him so dearly for one brief hour.

Time passed, and when he was grown, his father had let his heart grow bitter and cruel in useless grief and rebellion over the loss of his beautiful wife as well as through the disappointment in the heir to all his goods and lands.

One day, in an outburst of grief and rage, he said to his son: "You monster! You idiot! You shall pay dearly for making me ridiculous in the eyes of my attendants. You hunchback! If you knew how much your weakness and this eternal staring at the stars annoy me, you would find some other place in which to live!"

With these words burning in his heart, Selim went away trembling with fright and dismay. As he passed through his father's lands, even the peacocks of emerald and blue and bronze, on the wall of the garden of lilies, mocked at him with their ugly calls. He could still hear them when he was a long way off. As he came to a great forest, he suffered loneliness and despair because he, Selim, a Guiding Star, had

made his father, the Caliph, a laughing stock to
his attendants, and a shame to the house of Iblis.

He went into the depths of the forest of ban-
yan trees and of trees of the waving palm, where
the flamingo spreads its crimson wings, and
parrots talk incessantly. Toward evening under
a lofty tree, whereon a jasmine vine trailed in
tangled masses—a shower of dim and falling
stars—he lay as still as a sacred lotus blossom
on a sacred still pool, very sad and lonely, thinking over his misfortune. He had never as yet
seen himself, but always he had been told how
ugly he was, and how deformed.

While he was thus thinking, he heard the
sweetest music that ever an unfortunate youth
had heard. It was like a cluster of ring doves
and innumerable waterfalls, all in a perfect harmony, singing in a low murmuring sound, almost below their breath, a melody in words
that have lost their shadows and in words that
have lost their echoes.

He arose and followed the music until he
came to a myrtle grove intermingled with trees
hung with yellow fruit and bell-shaped flowers.
Over the ground, and hanging from the trees in
garlands, were vines of moon flowers. Like
a slim column of mist a fountain arose in the
midst, as though its water were seeking to lose
itself in the odour of the moon flowers.

The water looked so cool as it fell into the
pool, starred with firm round water lilies, that
he stooped down and drank, using his hands as
a cup. But even in this enchanted place, he
could not escape from his humiliation. Among
the flowers, pictured all quiveringly, he beheld
his likeness. He had, as yet, never seen his
ugly and deformed self, and he looked now for
the first time at his hunched back. He turned
away in despair.

As he turned he looked up at the clear, rising
stream of water. What was his amazement to
find that the fountain was flowing over a maiden,

· "WHAT · WAS · HIS · AMAZEMENT · TO · FIND · THAT · THE · FOUNTAIN ·
· WAS · FLOWING · OVER · A · MAIDEN" ·

whiter than the moon herself. Yellow water
lilies were in her black hair, falling with the
water of the fountain, and her flesh took on
opalescent gleams through the scarce-concealing
silky webs and veils of gossamer, the colour of
running water, now opaque, now transparent.

Never before had any one looked into his
eyes as she did. Others had always looked beyond, over his shoulder, at the hump on his'
back.

When he had looked into the maiden's eyes
as though it was forever, and yet as though it
were but for a moment, she came from the water,
holding out her hands. At her coming all the
air was perfumed with the delicate fragrance of a
shower of Spring falling upon jasmine blossoms.
In each hand she held a drop of water from the
fountain, which she placed upon the hump on
his back, and from out of it drew a casket of
ivory and coral, whereon were carved, in an intri-
cate design, stars and strange birds. It was

garlanded with waning moons and coral drops,
falling like bubbles, and over all, set deep in the
ivory, was a moonstone.

Holding it to her heart, she approached the
fountain, lingering over the water for a moment.
Then, advancing very gently toward him, she
looked searchingly into his eyes.

Next, she took a crystal globe from out the
casket, which, at a sign from her, they held between them. As they did so, their reflection
in the magic dewdrop became intermingled.
Selim, searching for the beauty of her face, saw,
but did not know it, the light of his own eyes.
She saw, reflected therein, the light of his pure
soul shining in his eyes, while, through the
potency of the magic sphere, he felt her love
and kindness beam upon him.

As they were thus looking at one another,
through their reflections, seeing what neither
had ever seen before. a solitary star cast its
poised and quivering light upon the crystal, like

an echo of the light of the love which had glowed upon him from his mother's eyes, when she held him to her heart for that one sweet hour.

A tear of joy fell on the Magic Dewdrop which broke as lightly as a bubble on the gentlest wind of June. And left them looking into one another's eyes. Then Selim the Hunchback straightway felt his crooked back change its shape, expand and become flexible; felt his legs grow straight. Behold! He was transformed into a beautiful youth.

Joy laughed in his eyes, deep happiness surged and flooded his heart, even as the tides of the full moon flood the shores of the sea. He ran to the trees and gathered apricots, cherries, and golden fruits, with the loveliest of the flowers, to give to the maiden of the fountain. She entwined a wreath of the yellow lilies about his hair. Taking his hand in hers, she led him to the fountain and showed him his reflection in the water, which was beautifully clear and still now. It was with wonder that he saw the marvelous change that had been wrought.

In his great joy, he cried to her: "O Star of my heart! O Star of my life! Since I have once seen you, I shall be able to think of nothing else; therefore, all the days of my life I will serve you. The magic of your loveliness has made me whole. Peace and happiness you have brought to my lonely heart and rejoicing to the house of Iblis. I shall bring you the richest fruits, and find you the fairest flowers. It is so sweet to be loved, so sweet—so sweet! O Star of the world! If I can only make you happy!"

Selim led the maiden to his father's gardens, whence he had fled in sorrow and dismay. At the sight of his erect and youthful beauty, and the soft radiance of the fair maiden at his side, all who had once mocked him, now ran to do him honour. A troop of black slaves received them, throwing themselves on the ground at their feet. An especially arrayed slave, with bands of orange and crimson silk about his waist, and great copper rings swinging from his ears, ran before them to tell the Caliph. Filled with gratitude, the father raised his hands to Ormuzd the Blessed, to give thanks.

Then on every side were heard strains of music as Selim and the maiden, more lovely and more radiant than all the stars, appeared before the Caliph. The brilliancy of the lilies in their hair was such that they outshone the sun itself. The Caliph bowed his head and wept for happiness.

Amid great rejoicing over all the land of Iblis, on that very day was the wedding celebrated. After there had been a great feast, the Caliph led the youthful lovers to the most beautiful rooms in the palace, which had been set apart for them. There at the foot of the maiden's couch, perfumed with musk and the dry petals of roses, Selim lay on a carpet of cloth of gold embroidered with innumerable stars and birds.

He told her stories about her eyes. He said they were like deep, dark pools that mirrored the reflection of the sky on a Summer night, sparkling with a million lights. He told her about her forehead which was like a shell-tinted ivory, bathed in the moonlight of May. When he had finished the story of her great beauty, he again started with her eyes, and told it all over and over again. Indeed, he was never tired of telling, nor she of listening to, the story of his great love.

On a night when the flower-petals fell, heavy with dripping dew, when the night birds had sung their last song and the dove's cooing was hushed in the sweetest sleep, Selim and the maiden walked together in the moon-silvered garden of the lilies, and talked of their love. Selim said:

"O pure and beautiful one!—mounting in splendour over the horizon of my youth, like a radiant star, to cast the sweetness of your love over all the days of my life!—tell me, I pray you, whence did you come?"

She answered: "My mother bore me under a blooming tree when the moon was on the wane, and died with the fading of the stars. There, too, would I have perished of cold and hunger, had not Mirtas of the silver hair found me. I lived always in his little house in a forest of singing birds and sweet-scented flowers. At evening I spent the happiest hours, listening to the tales of magic that Mirtas told me.

"He told me of the Dewdrop which the great and beautiful Queen had found, and of the Caliph's son, who had a hump on his back, but eyes in which ever shone the light of a star. When Mirtas had grown old, and death was near, he confined me in the fountain by spells of magic.

"Then said Mirtas: 'Here must you stay, a child of running water, until a youth comes. When you have seen the image of a star shining in his eyes, he will claim you for his bride.'

"In your eyes, O Selim, my heart, my lover, my Guiding Star, I saw a gleam like that reflected in the Dewdrop that your dear mother found in the heart of the lily whose face looked up to the Heaven,—the Magic Dewdrop, for which Ormuzd's name be praised."

COLD PORRIDGE

COLD PORRIDGE

"The Man in the Moon
Came tumbling down,
And asked the way
to Norwich;
He went by the south
And burned his mouth
With eating cold
pease porridge."

IN THE red-roofed and white-gabled houses that were crowded together in the streets of So-and-So Town there was not a window that did not have at least one head leaning from the casement as far as it was safe to lean. There was not a mouth of one of the faces looking into the narrow streets of So-and-So Town whose lips were not moving as fast as lips can move, and some faster than lips should. Every person who lived within the narrow houses was quarreling with his next-door neighbour, or his neighbour two doors removed, and some were calling in loud, angry voices to those who dwelt across the street.

Window after window had opened in the square and in the narrow streets that radiated from the market place as a centre and led far away to the hills and valleys with their cornfields, farms, and vineyards.

"Shut up that noise," angrily shouted Horner, the tanner, as his white-capped head emerged from a window.

"My good friend, *you* shut up, yourself," said Solomon Shaftoe, severely.

"I must have my sleep," cried old Jenny Linnet, as she tipped her candle. The grease dropped on Thomas Stroat's shining red nose, which had appeared from a window two stories below.

"Give us our rest," shouted the crowd.

"Fiddle-come-fie, what is all the chatter about?" inquired old Rook, the tinker.

"Sleep! Sleep! Sleep!" yelled everybody excitedly.

"Who is moaning that way this time of night?" inquired the thick-headed Clint, and when no answer came he swore at nobody at all.

"Can't you show a little straight common sense?" yelled Muffet, as he spat out of his window.

"You filthy swine!" shouted a hoarse voice, wagging his head.

"You lazy loon," came from a garret window. The owner of this voice did not know to whom he was addressing this remark, but that did not make any difference.

Someone intended making an end of the noise but a fit of coughing choked him before he could speak. He cursed shrilly between coughs.

"Shut up that noise!"

"Shut up, yourself, you disturber of the peace."

"La, how the world wags!" said old Grundy, wrapping a shawl around his throat. The children cried, and one dog, and then another, barked.

In the back yard of Weevil, the pieman, a yellow hound sat on his haunches and joined in the din. He was indifferent to the sounds about him; he was baying at the moon, two nights from the full, as it peeped over his master's wall, sending a stream of light into the kitchen and lighting the shelves whereon were innumerable tarts and a bowl of curd and whey.

There was no one to blame. No townsman had said a word or done a deed to cause a quarrel with his neighbour. Indeed, it was not a man that walks on this earth who had awakened all the sleeping people of So-and-So Town and started the chattering, grumbling, and scolding. It was the Man in the Moon who had recently paid a visit to Norwich and continued his journey southward, the smiling silver gentleman of the Moon who often paid visits to his friends in Norwich town. He was the unconscious disturber of the peaceful folk who lived in the little group of houses huddled together in a valley.

Now before the village was annoyed, in those days when the moon had been a new moon, the seeds of the trouble had been sown.

Timothy, the chandler, looked up from the tallow and over his left shoulder at the crescent. He wished he would be spared chilblains when the nights turned cold. Across the road, Martin, the son of the tinsmith, asked his sister for one more rhyme. Joan told him about

> "The Man in the Moon
> Came tumbling down,
> And asked the way
> to Norwich.
> He went by the south
> And burned his mouth,
> With eating cold
> pease porridge."

Little Martin liked this rhyme more than any one his sister had said for him. He asked her to say it again and again until he could repeat it without a mistake. He said it for Jill, the tanner's wife, and for Giles, the landlord of the inn. Jill told it to Jenny, the weaver's daughter; she in return repeated it to Clint, the cob-

bler, who told it to all the people who had
their shoes and boots repaired, and as fast as
they could discard the old boots and put on
the mended ones, they went on their way telling the rhyme to everyone they met.

By the time the moon was at the first quarter,
all who dwelt in So-and-So Town had said the
rhyme once, and many of them said it over and
over again for no reason at all.

Each felt it his duty to repeat it to his neighbours save Thrush, the lame boy, who lived in
a house by the side of a stream, lonely in situa-
tion; in fact, it was a quarter of the way between
the village and the woods.

By the house was the highroad gate. Thrush's
father opened and shut the gate for all who
passed through and they gave him a coin.

The lame boy had not heard the rhyme about
the Man in the Moon's visit to Norwich and so
he could not repeat it to any one. Therefore,
he sailed his little boat in the stream, that

widened here into a pond, as it ran past his
father's cottage. Back and forth from the port
of a large boulder on the edge of the water to
the harbour, which was safe within the shadow
of a bunch of Michaelmas daisies, the craft
Arrow made its perilous voyages just as though
the whole town were not talking about the Man
in the Moon's mouth.

The sleeplessness that had prevailed through-
out So-and-So Town had been started by the
rhyme. The Man in the Moon peeped into the
lighted windows of the houses as he journeyed
from the east to the west. He heard everyone
repeating the verse of a feast of porridge of
which he had partaken in Norwich. He had
visited Norwich, that was true, but he could not
remember if the porridge had been hot or cold.
Indeed he could not recall the porridge at all.

What man, whether he be on the earth or in
the moon, could resist the temptation of being
the hero of a rhyme? And so he waxed large

as fast as he was capable of waxing, and listened with a pleased smile to his heart's content. The rhyme that everyone was saying was not true. That fact did not affect any one but himself. He had not eaten the pease in Norwich. Indeed, he had never tasted porridge in his whole life. It is never found on the tables of the best moon families.

Long ago his mother had forbidden him to open his mouth. She told him if he parted his lips his teeth of ice would drop out and destroy the world and the stars. He liked to look into all the bright windows in the houses on earth, and he was very fond of watching the twinkling stars. Nothing would induce him to dim their lights. Therefore, even if the rhyme of which he was the hero were true, he was helpless to deny it. A good son he was and would not disobey his mother. Listening at every window-ledge for the rhyme, he followed the villagers straggling homeward through the streets, as they gleefully sang of his cold porridge. He listened to them until they shut their doors in his face.

He made the nights short on the other side of the world in order that he might again and again hear the rhyme in which he was the hero.

One night the moon stood halfway up the eastern sky shining very soft and yellow. The Moon pays all his visits to the earth in reflections although they can only be seen by others when there is still water or a window or a tear, but he is still present even if we cannot see him.

On this night the unseen reflection crept through the ordered rows of cabbages and turnips to a window where a dim light burned. Within, Joe Pye, the butcher, and his family were sitting around the supper table. The porridge pot was empty. The knives and forks lay crossed on the plates. Posey, the daughter of

Pye, was repeating the rhyme for a wandering clockmaker, who had stopped there for the night.

> " He went by the south,
> And burned his mouth "

she sang gaily as though it were amusing to burn the mouth on cold porridge.

When the Moon heard this the right corner of his mouth began to throb with a dull pain that hurt like toothache. As he crossed the sky the pain increased. Before midnight he thought he could not endure the suffering. He began to groan, a little noise he could make without parting his lips and disobeying his mother. Moaning seemed to help his suffering, and so, at regular intervals, he made a noise like humming, with grunts mixed in. It seemed a little noise to him, but the people on the worlds near by looked at the sky and said: "There will be a storm."

On his journey across the sky he searched for reflected images of himself in order that he might see how severely his mouth was scorched. In lakes and ponds where the water was calm and in windows where there was no light he looked at his reflection, to see if he could discover the burn of which everyone was singing.

Down into wells and springs he looked and in rain pools that lay in the road. He even searched for miniature portraits of himself in dewdrops that hung from the petals of wild flowers.

His path led him to the stream that ran by the side of the gatekeeper's house. On the edge of the water, tethered to a stalk of Michaelmas daisies, there was the little boat, made of a discarded spool box. Its gay sail was fashioned of yellow paper, stuck through a twig of hazel.

He was absorbed, in spite of the pain, by his honey-coloured image lying in the water. Here he could see his reflection and examine his lips.

Nowhere on this image could he find a sign of a burn on his pale mouth. Then a scarlet leaf from a maple branch that hung out and over the pond fell on the water where his reflection was. The leaf distorted the smooth surface of the stream and made a gay smile on his lips when he felt none in his heart.

In spite of his failure to discover the burn on his lips, he continued to moan. Everyone said he had burned his mouth on cold porridge and even if he could not see the scorched place it must be there, for someone, perchance it was a poet, had made a rhyme about it.

And so it was that all the people of So-and-So Town had been kept awake for several nights, The annoyance developed, as you have seen, into a general altercation, which has been keeping up without ceasing all of the time that you have been learning the causes and reasons for the strange sounds.

"Shut up that noise," everyone was shouting at everyone else.

"Peter and Paul, save us," said Noel from a low window, "to-morrow is wash day."

While Money, from a high window, shook his fist as he yelled at everybody, "Can't you let a man sleep?"

"Shut up!"

"Shut up!"

"What is it all about?" mumbled Mall, the grandmother of ten, as she drew in her ear trumpet from outside the window.

Presently from the far end of the square, by the inn, came the sound of cheering. Next the loud voice of the town crier rose above the clatter of some nine hundred voices shouting, complaining, howling, and cursing.

"Oyez! Oyez! Oyez! Be patient, good neighbours. If ye have reason, go back to your beds and sleep. The occasion is very urgent that ye get your rest. For it is commanded by the mayor that to-morrow, one and all of you townsfolk meet at the market place. We will decide without delay how the dismal noise can be hushed!"

The riot began anew. Grumbling, beseeching, and cursing issued forth from every window.

"Wait until to-morrow!" one shouted.

"Faugh! No sleep to-night," said another.

But one and all did sleep. The moon turned yellow and sank out of sight behind the hills in the west. The town and the fields were dark. The stars shone brighter in the sky. Soon only the regular snores of a fat baker came from the window of Weevil. Jenny Linnet's candle spluttered and flickered out. She had fallen asleep before she could snuff it. The yellow hound stopped baying, since there was no longer a moon to bay at; he slept with his nose pressed against his master's door.

Next morning the people began streaming up to the market place of So-and-So Town at an

early hour. Wren, a ploughman, had told the
the gatekeeper's wife Mary of the affair before
the spool-box boat *Arrow* had made its second
voyage from the large rock to the Michaelmas
daisies.

Thrush's father could not go to the meeting
in the market place as the mayor had bidden
all the good townsfolk lest one traveller should
pass through the gates without leaving his
toll.

So Mary went slowly to the market place with
the lame child's hand in hers as he limped by
her side. Sometimes she stopped, sat down by
the roadside, and took him on her lap. He
could not walk so fast as the others and had to
rest often because of the only hurt place she
could not make all well with kisses. As they
drew near the square, a low muttering now made
itself heard, rising to a roar that seemed to fill the
place. The market was overflowing with the
whole population. They jostled each other

along the sides of it, chattering, shoving, and
ordering everyone else to stand back, and each
one standing as far forward himself as he could.
Mary kept on the edge of the crowd until she
came to the steps of the cobbler's house, where
she stood and watched, keeping the lame boy
close beside her.

Soon in the centre of the square, the mayor,
a great blunt man with red hair, commanded
silence by uplifted hands. Then he said in a
husky voice:

"God's peace, good people! The dreadful noise
must be hushed and the nights left for rest and
sleep. If you will be patient until the council
meets, they will decide what is best to be done."

The council met for an hour in the council
house. Their faces were long and thin, and
they sat with their heads on one side, thinking
and thinking, their eyes fastened on the ground.
When the hour had passed the people of So-and-
So Town were more perplexed than they had

been before the council met. If they had failed
to discover the source of the moaning and
groaning, surely it was impossible to put an end
to the noise. Since the meeting of the council
had left the problem unsolved, seven of the
wisest men of the town came together in a
conference. But no sooner did they gather
than they one and all wanted to show their wisdom. However learned they were, their knowledge proved insufficient.

In spite of much valiant talk, no one was
found wise enough to free the suffering village
of the nights of restlessness. Each hour the
heated discussions ended in nothing.

Now while the council was meeting and the
wise men were displaying their wisdom, Mary
sat in the shop of Clint, the cobbler, who was
cobbling her shoes. While she was waiting,
Betty Pye stopped for a bit of gossip and Posey
played at jackstones with Thrush on the door
step. The little girl told the lame boy the

rhyme about The Man in the Moon and his poor aching mouth.

All the meetings over, the townsfolk congregated in the square. Again the mayor raised his hands and said:

"My good people we have faithfully debated —H'um"—(he tossed his head); "the only thing we all can agree on is this: that this sort of thing cannot be allowed to go on. Who it is that makes the noise, and how it is to be stopped, no one can discover."

Thrush, the lame boy, who had apparently been gazing with childish interest at the red face of one of the council, gave a sudden cry of understanding. After he had drawn his mother's face down and had whispered in her ear, he limped, with the aid of his crutch, toward the mayor.

"What is he doing?" asked one.

"What is Mary thinking about?" exclaimed another.

There was a low murmur as the crowd moved

toward the boy. Thrush limped one step nearer
the mayor and paused. He looked up into his
eyes, unafraid, as he quoted:

"The Man in the Moon
Came tumbling down,
And asked the way
to Norwich.
He went by the south
And burned his mouth
With eating cold
pease porridge."

Then Thrush, who had never lacked love and
devotion and sympathy to help him bear his
own affliction, added with his childlike earnest-
ness, touched by pity:

"The poor moon hasn't anybody to kiss his
mouth and make it all well again."

The councillors were awestruck. Two of
them giggled together, another complained of
chilly feet and spat. The mayor had heard
the rhyme, and he had said it. Now that he
thought about it, the moaning had occurred only
at night and the moon was almost at the full.
Why had he not thought of that himself?

First of all he was angry; and then over his large round face there stole a smile. He nodded his head at the little boy.

"He is right; the boy is right," he chuckled. "Someone must kiss the Man in the Moon and make him well. The poor fellow has burned his mouth."

But who was tall enough to reach up and kiss him? No one could touch his lips even if one stood on the highest house. Again the council was summoned. Together with all the wise and learned men they retired behind the doors of the council house.

There were the usual discussions and results. Then followed a long silence that was broken by someone yawning. A middle-aged man with a certain subdued drollery in his face stood in his black velvet and fur. He cleared his throat and said:

"The Man in the Moon is suffering from a burned mouth. A burned mouth is very pain-

ful. I once received a burn on my wrist as I
was taking a duck out of the oven for my wife.
The moon's groans have disturbed our sleep
and now the town is at the point of a riot if
something is not done to stop the noise. Birds
fly. If a man had wings why could he not fly
like a bird? Let us make a pair of wings.
Choose a man with sense who can reach the
moon and kiss the burned place."

There was a low murmur of approval over the
meeting of wise and learned councillors. And
the men who were afraid to be simple adjourned
to carry out their plans.

Within an hour every inhabitant of So-and-So
Town was running after birds, butterflies, dragonflies, moths, beetles, bees, and all creatures that
possess wings.

The women gathered in a circle under the
mulberry trees in the square. While some of
them made the frames of twigs and branches,
others spun and wove the little broken wings

and feathers into a covering for the framework, crowding them together like the feathers on a bird's wing.

A line of yellow butterflies' pinions, then a line of dragonflies' wings were strung on a scarlet thread. A circle of the shining wings of hornets, wasps, and bees was placed here, and a star of white moths' wings there, then a broad line of cardinals' feathers between the breast feathers of humming birds, most beautifully arranged and producing a harmony of colour and shade.

"Oh, they are beautiful!" exclaimed some. Others added: "Quite charming."

"Magnificent!" exclaimed the mayor, looking at them through his spectacles. "Such a pattern! And these colours! The wings have my highest approval!"

"They are wonderful."

"Gorgeous!"

"Excellent," went from mouth to mouth.

They were all equally delighted with their handiwork.

And so the feathers on a thousand throats ceased to swell with a song because of a rhyme pertaining to a pot of porridge. And a thousand hearts ceased their tremulous beat for the sake of a burn on a silver mouth.

While the framework was being adorned and approved, the councilmen went through the streets, telling the youths and men of the great adventure in prospect. There was not one among them who did not wish to be chosen to soar aloft into the sky and kiss the lips of the Man in the Moon, to say nothing of the bag of gold that had been offered as a reward for restoring to the people of So-and-So Town their calm and restful nights.

Lots were drawn from the mayor's hat. As the last feather from a goldfinch's breast was stitched on the large false wings, Bardolph, the growing son of the widow Moll, drew forth from the hat a scrap of blue paper whereon was written the winner's number. He clapped his hands gleefully.

The magnificent flight was to be made an hour after the Man in the Moon rose over the roofs of the houses that surrounded the square.

Far across the fields of stubble that lay to the east of So-and-So Town, a yellow moon, approaching the full, rose slowly, fading the stars and lighting with a cool light the fields where the sheaves of corn stood.

Bardolph, the goat-herd, was sunburned and comely, very tall, and his deep pool-like eyes were as tender as a wild-flower. When the marvellous wings were fastened to his arms at the wrist and elbow with broad strings of leather, and the harness that held them in place was strapped over his chest, he went to his mother. For a moment his head lay upon her breast. She caressed the golden hair ever so lightly, and tenderly kissed him upon the lips.

Now having kissed his mother again and again, he said: "I will be sorry to leave my goats." Then he started away with a quick stiff stride.

Bardolph ran to the Town Hall, ascended to the roof, and crawled out to the gables. Here he stood, balancing against the weather vane that gleamed pale in the moonlight. The wings flashed clear as he stood for a second against the sky. The youth was now filled with a great glow of exultation and looked like an angel carved from weather-worn silver.

Smiling, he turned and gazed at his mother, then smiled into the people's upturned faces. Spreading the huge wings he saluted with them four times. Once to the north and once to the south, once to the east, and once to the west.

Then Bardolph gave a triumphant shout and flung himself into the air.

His wrists fell and the only son of the widow Moll shot down the air and lay crushed and limp like a slain bird.

The crowd had moved aside when the wings
gave way so that no one was crushed beneath the
heart that had ceased its youthful throbbing for
the sake of a song concerning a burned mouth.
There was a cry of dismay and the next moment
you might have heard a long, awed murmur go
about the market place as the crowd of people
watching caught its breath. The mother uttered
a cry of despair. She sank upon her knees
hiding her face and moaning as she cried: "He
said he would be sorry to leave his goats." The
women fell to sobbing in one another's arms so
piteously, that the sturdy middle-aged townsfolk
drew back and were ashamed.

The dew was falling, the night ending in So-
and-So Town. The yellow hound kept up his
nightly baying in the back yard of Weevil, the
pieman. The moon, silver and nearly full, hung
in the sky, solitary, in his imagined suffering.
He had not seen the tragedy that had befallen
the widow Moll that night in the market place

of So-and-So Town. When it occurred he was looking at a miniature of himself reflected in a dewdrop clinging to the petal of a white balsam that drooped in a pot. The flower stood on a ledge outside of the widow Moll's window. Therefore, he did not know why the moisture was in old Moll's eyes, when he looked through the window later and saw his smiling face reflected in a tear. Even in that miniature portrait of himself in a broken-hearted mother's eye, he could not discover the burn on his lips, which had become well nigh unbearable by this time because of the constant thinking thereon, and so he continued his regular moans.

For an hour the next morning the councillors sat again in council. The mayor advanced to the council table. He said in a toneless voice:

"This is the worst thing that could happen to me. Am I not fit for my post? Cannot one of you wise men put an end to the pest?"

Every one of these men who were afraid to be

natural shook a slow and steady "No" to his plea. The mayor, followed by the councillors, marched to the centre of the square and asked the people if there was not one among them who could suggest a plan whereby the village might find peace. Many suggestions were here offered and plans made but all of no avail. Until the sun began to sink behind the hills and the birds twittered in the tree tops, the mayor stood in the square considering one plan after another. Then he sent forth one more appeal to the people of So-and-So Town for help in this serious matter.

Mary, the gate-keeper's wife, was returning home again. The journey to the gate-house was long and the road would soon be dark. As she passed by the mayor, Thrush limped at his mother's side, clasping her hand.

"I can make him well, Mother," he said earnestly.

"You," cried his mother, another mother's

tragedy before her eyes, "and what do you think you could do about it, my little boy?"

"It is only a burn on his lip," replied the boy quietly. "You know when I bump my head you can make it all well again if you kiss it. I'll talk to him. All these people don't understand him a bit. He gets his feelings hurt." He told his mother what he thought he could do and she told the mayor.

"Let the boy alone," he declared, "I am not quite sure but that he is right. He makes friends with everybody. He'll find out what the poor fellow needs."

After the mother had told the mayor the boy's thoughts, he gave his consent to anything that might bring rest, and added a few suggestions to the lad's plan.

"Give him a trial," the mayor said commandingly to the councillors, "I like the boy, there is a brave light in his eyes."

"Please leave it all to me," commanded Thrush,

"I'll make him all well to-night. Only please don't let any one say another word about the Man in the Moon's mouth."

Thrush found it an easy matter to set his mother at ease about his plan. She always took his word without a murmur although she suggested that the boy take some soda and clean linen with him for the burned spot.

It was a crisp autumn night. The air was filled with the odour of burning leaves and brush. The Moon at its full would soon come over the sea of rolling hills. All the folk of So-and-So Town were gathered in the square waiting for the promised event.

Soon Thrush's crutch began to knock on the stones of the walk. After him came his mother with the mayor and the councillors. The crowd formed in a procession and silently followed the limping boy. They kept at a respectful distance behind the councillors who walked two by two.

· "THE LITTLE · BOY · KISSED · THE · SPOT · AND · MADE · IT · · ALL WELL " ·

On and on through the town they marched and out into the fields, over dry rustling leaves and falling twigs that cracked beneath their feet. Past the fields to the hill slopes Thrust led them.

The people below saw him stop when he reached the top of the highest hill. They whispered to each other that he had dropped his crutch and that he seemed to stand very still against the sky, waiting.

Then the bald silver head of the moon rose over the crest of the hill that seemed like the edge of the world. To the eager watchers below the boy was a little sharp-cut shape against the bright light of the moon's forehead.

"Good evening, Man," they heard Thrush say politely, between the groans of the moon.

The Man raised his eyebrows and made a different sort of noise.

"I have come up here to see how you are and to make you all well," continued the boy.

The large eyes smiled courteously. Thrush

dropped on his knees. His lips seemed to touch the ivory cheek as the crowd saw the corner of the smiling mouth rise over the hill-tops.

From all sides, that still evening, could be heard the quick breathing of the mothers.

The miracle had been accomplished. The Moon's moans and groans ceased. Had not Thrush, the little boy, kissed the spot and made it all well?

A gracious and gentle smile of gratitude spread over the Moon's amber face as it rose higher and higher in the sky. Amid joyful shouts, shrill cries of women and children, little Thrush the lame son of the Gatekeeper sat still, filled with the power that can exist in the silence of a child.

OUT OF DOORS

WAITING DREAMS

THERE is a pool in the Sand-man's garden
wherein he cools those dreams that must
rest on lovely ladies' eyes on summer nights, and
where he washes those dreams that grow dusty
while they are waiting to be delivered.

There are many of these, as all the dreams
wherein there is any love have to be made in
the dawns and twilights of spring, even though
they must lie on the shelves for a year. They are
all very sweet and fragile and attract the dust from
moths' and butterflies' wings, and particularly
do they allure the pollen of certain flowers.

Sometimes those that contain a kiss are even
found coated with mist. This, as you must
surely know, is star dust. The Sand-man pre-
serves it to make dreams for mothers.

And we who are not mothers can never have
them!

A FAIRY RING TO VALENTINE

WHEN a fairy feels himself falling in love, if perchance there has been a light, fresh fall of snow, he climbs up the stem of a blowing blade of grass, which bends to the earth beneath his weight. When persuaded by the varying, playing breezes, the grass blade traces a ring around him in the snow, he knows good fortune is his, and flies forth to woo his Fairy Love in some deserted milkweed seedpod wherein perchance she dwells.

I pray that the good Saint of this day will trace a fairy ring around me, that good fortune may be mine as I start on a quest for the place wherein you dwell, O my Valentine, wherever in the wide world you may be! When I have found you and looked into your eyes, may dear Saint Valentine inscribe around you and me the circle of lasting love.

· "A · FRAGILE · CRAFT, · PILOTED · BY · A · FAIRY, · PERCHED ·
· LIKE · A · STAR" ·

ON JUNE WINDS

LIFT up your heads, all ye who sigh for summer, for from their silken ports have set sail
the odour-laden fleet. Soon to you, on the waves
of the south wind, will come the scented vessels
bearing their precious cargoes and spilling them
recklessly.

O fragrance of heliotrope, mimosa, and mignonette!

The fragile crafts are piloted by a fairy
perched like a star, holding the cobweb cables
from the mist-like, winging sails. Above, a
figurehead tells of coming sweetness, waving
silken petals as they are brushed by the rippling
breeze.

So lift up your heads, ye sighers for the summer, breathe in your fill of their perfume as it
blows against your cheek. Sweetly it touches

you with its soft caresses, the lingering fresh-
ness pervading everything. And then, swiftly
it is gone, murmuring only to the bees the
name of the harbour which is home.

TO MY GROWN-UP SELF

ALL the days of my life as I sat dreaming on the fountain of my youth I dreamed of that day when you would come. The blooming of springtime over the garden of my youth where the fountain ever sang itself into circles that spread around the lilies of the pool, told me your coming was near. And when the immortal peacock that had dreamed all its life on the fountain of my youth had awakened from its dreams and preened the feathers of its breast, I was afraid that the peacock would never dream again, and the fountain's plashing waters would cease to hold the lilies in its ceaseless circles, and I would lose the dreams one dreams only at the fountain of life's springtime.

But when spring had come and you had sat beside me at the fountain of my youth, in your eyes I found youth immortal: for together we could dream with the peacock on the margin of your fountain and mine.

163

SNAPDRAGONS

IN THE world of hot and windless summer days, it is watering time for the thirsting flock of pink and yellow dragons, whose fiercest flights are their gentle swayings back and forth as they are caressed by summer breezes.

Down through the summer night, on soundless wings, the fairies of the starlight make their way, each bearing a goblet of dew from out the fountains of the air. And when the fairies have reached the end of their pathless flight, resting on still wings they press the dragon's silken sides.

Eagerly he snaps his fragile mouth wide to receive the cooling drink, as the fairies tip the goblet, and spill the dew from out the fountains that play incessantly, perhaps on some remote star.

: "IT · IS · WATERING · TIME · FOR · THE · THIRSTING · FLOCK · OF ·
· PINK · AND · YELLOW · DRAGONS" ·

AS POSTED BY LEGAL
AUTHORITY

A REWARD of fourteen dreams will be given for information leading to the arrest and conviction of those persons guilty of starting the unjust and unkind rumour:

> "Lady bug, Lady bug, fly away home,
> Your house is on fire and your children
> will burn."

I THE undersigned, Shrimpie Snippet, am related to Lady bugs. I am so nearly related that I have never heard the fire alarms yet that I did not fly—not home; Alas! I have no home to which to fly, no children have I to burn. But as fast as I can, do I run to the Lady bug's home that is reported burning.

I SHRIMPIE SNIPPET, own a Lady bug all of my own. To make her walk forward, you must make her walk backward ten steps, then she will walk forward twenty steps. If you try to make her walk forward before she has walked backward ten steps, she will stand still and never walk forward or backward again.

THEREFORE, am not I, Shrimpie Snippet, right in endeavouring to discover the miscreant who is the cause of so much unrest, so much uneasiness, so much agitation against my dear kinspeople, the Lady bugs?

AND possessing a Lady bug, as I do, who will walk forward in proper Lady bug fashion, if she is made to walk backward ten steps before she starts forward, have not I, Shrimpie Snippet, every right to try to put an end to this upsetting gossip?

Signed: SHRIMPIE SNIPPET.

SWEET APRIL

APRIL! my silver-sandled sister, your singing comes to me on the first wave of the spring's warming wind. Soon over the green earth will you dance right merrily, with hoops of singing birds swinging from your ears. The silent shadows of these singing birds are as bracelets around your arms that wave, first this way (making the daffodils unfold their shining faces), and then that way (breaking the sweet bird's egg and sending forth a bonny song).

I have waited so long, my sister—sister April—since my true love left me; with you I need to dance. When buds are breaking and birds singing merrily, dance with me, dance with me to the ripple of the rain. As over your golden path we move so lightly, let my arms wave with yours that I, too, may break one sweet blue egg.

My heart will throb with gladness if I can free one song for summer. And perhaps I, who must remember, will forget that my love has left me, and has forgotten that I must live through a silver-scented spring.

"WHEN · BUDS · ARE · BREAKING · AND · BIRDS : SINGING · · MERRILY, · DANCE · WITH · ME"

ALONE

ALL silently out into a summer night leaned a little moonflower on the very border-land of birth.

With a sigh softer than the stirring of a bird-ling within a blue egg, it said, from its infolded self, so soft, so sweet:

"Forth from my heart I shall send a wealth of pure white petals. I shall keep them so in-nocent and spotless that as a beacon against the night they will gleam like a star.

"I shall breathe forth such a fragrance of sorrowful sweetness that it will lure the loveliest of the butterflies—blue patterned on gold, gold on ivory—to come to me and sip his fill of my silver honey."

The little bloom in a moon-moulded nativity, all expectantly unfolded frail light petals, revealing itself as pure as a baby's palm, wistfully sweet.

Trembling on a fragile stem it forced itself beyond the embrace of the tendrils of the moon-flower vine. But only a moth came and sojourned within its sweetness until the setting of the stars.

When dawn had laid a purple light over the garden wide, the lonely little flower folded a vanquished heart deep within drooping petals and was about to die. Then the butterfly of its ivory and blue and gold dream came to gather the ravaged treasure.

But so assuredly had it enwrapped fading petals around its heart that not even all the stars of another summer night could unveil its silken sadness.

A LITTLE DREAM THAT WANDERED

LOST, Strayed, or Stolen:
On Easter Eve, from Littleboy Lovelock's garden, a Dream.

Small and shaped like the bulb of a lily, made of April's melted snowflakes, and April's first buds, and the down from under baby birds' wings.

This dream was designed for a baby girl born on Easter Day, and was to be the first she ever had. All the years of her life it was to have been repeated on the night preceding her birthday.

If returned to Littleboy Lovelock before this baby is fourteen days old the finder will be rewarded with a dream of a waterfall, a singing bird, and a blooming tree.

171

If not returned and the dream is found in any one's possession, he or she will be inflicted with a dream that will make him or her think that he or she has measles, mumps, and "getting mad"-ness at one and the same time.

SUMMER BREEZES

OVER the hills and through the valleys Summer strays with her scarf of light winds, and, with utter sweetness, caresses the weeds and flowers, blessing every blossom with a precious drink of dew, while Winter draws his garment of frost around him and stands remotely aside, silently waiting for something beautiful to happen.

With her scarf blowing against our faces, Summer gives to each of us her gift of bird and bee and bloom.

AUTUMN'S COLOUR

ALL the days of my life I have roamed the world over in quest of the rainbow's end —"where" (a wise man said) "you will find a pot of gold, filled to the brim and overflowing."

Alas, I cannot find it!

And so, to stay at home and be content, I listened to the fairies (they are wiser than the wisest man in the whole world), and I believe them when they tell me what I would have found had I reached the end of my quest:

"At the end of the rainbow there is not a pot of gold, but seven great pots brimming over with colours. Up in the air, on the other side of the wide, wide world, a fountain is silently playing: first red; then orange; afterward yellow and green; blue, then indigo and violet.

"The rainbow is the colour spilling from the

· "WHENCE · DO · THE · ELVES · GET · ALL · THE · COLOUR ·
· THEY · NEED · WITH · WHICH · TO · PAINT · THE ·
· FLOWERS, · FRUITS · AND · FOLIAGE ?" ·

fountain's seven basins and flowing in circled paths across the sky into the brims of the waiting pots."

If this is not true, pray tell me, whence do the elves of the autumn get all the colour they need with which to paint the flowers, fruits, and foliage?

LITTLE BIRDS

ONCE upon a time there was a boy named Dickie Dear who tried very hard to make himself grow up. But try as hard as he might, he could not succeed.

Nowhere in the whole wide world could he find the adventure he thought he wanted, but really did not need at all.

Now this Dickie Dear lived in a little brown house, which half of the day lay in the shadow of a tall, gray church steeple. Up in the belfry lived families of birds, and in the vines that grew between the windows of the church lived other families of birds. Through all the dawns of winter this boy named Dickie Dear listened to the chattering of the birds—those delightful chatterings that always occur in families that live in nests and little brown houses which lie in the shadow of gray church steeples. Through all the noons in spring, Dickie Dear watched the building of new bird-homes and listened to the chattering of the busy families.

One day a man came to paint the window-frames of the church, and he began his work by pulling down the vines wherein these chattering families had built new homes. The boy named Dickie Dear rushed out of the little brown house which lay in the shadow of the gray church steeple, and he ran over to the man, who was only doing what he had been told to do. But Dickie Dear was too late! The homes were all destroyed; the chattering babies lay squashed in the shadow of the tall church steeple!

Dickie Dear came back to the little brown house, and, because he was very, very unhappy, shut the door very, very hard, which shook the little brown house, and made some of his play-things fall off the shelves whereon they were wont to stand.

On one shelf, through the dawns of winter and the noons of spring, had stood a lonely doll. He had travelled all the way from China! Of course, he was a heathen Chinaman, but very good for all that. Now this Chinaman, with the other toys, had fallen off the shelf and lay on the floor with his head thrown out of the hole in his blue coat where one's head should always be.

Dickie Dear felt very sorry for all his toys, but he was sorriest for the Chinaman, for he knew it must be very unpleasant to have one's head out of place. So he picked up the Chinaman, put his head in the hole of his coat where heads usually grow, and stood him in his rightful place upon the shelf.

Ever since the Chinaman had arrived from China he had not spoken a single word, but this painful adventure—for a certain reason which I really cannot explain—made him sing. Not being a Chinaman, I cannot sing the song as he did, but this is how it sounded to me:

"Dickie, dear boy, don't be sad for the little birds that lie squashed in the shadow of the great gray church. A moment ago I lay squashed upon the floor. Just as you have made me as I was, so Some One makes the little birds just as they were. You see me as I was because I am only a heathen Chinaman, but you cannot see the little birds as they were because One who guards each of His little children as you have guarded me, has made them little birds again in a golden world called Paradise."

DREAM BOATS—
PLAY

DREAM BOATS—
PLAY

PRELUDE

PLAYFELLOWS

Robin Ringlet

Davy—the little boy

A Prologue

An Alien-kinsman to the Fairies

A Sea-horse

You

You *are sitting in the left-hand box. Now sit up in a proper fashion as though you have escorted two lovely ladies to see the play.* You, *over there, are sitting in the parquet and* You *are in the first balcony. Everyone else is in the peanut gallery. I am glad you are because you can eat peanuts. I am the actors. I hope you will like me.*

183

The scenery for the play is a picture inside a picture frame showing two boats drifting on a Summer sea at moonrise. The figure-head on the first boat is a feather from a white peacock's tail. A large quivering bubble serves as a figurehead for the second boat which is drifting in the wake the first boat leaves in the water behind it.

Before the rise of the theatre curtain enter from the left A PROLOGUE. *He crosses to the centre of the stage, carefully turning out his toes.*

A Prologue. This is not a play because the author (who wrote it) is not a playwright. Therefore, it is not a play.

It is better than a play, for you have to come to play with us and we are going to play with you. Therefore, it is play-play-play!

He pauses, looks quickly and suddenly to the right and to the left.

A Prologue. All the babies that come into this

world hold something in their tiny hands. All Mothers know that, but few realize that the little fingers are clasping with all their might and main the invisible key to the Magic Casement. In some way nearly every baby learns (I believe it is whispered to them by nurse maids) the delightful things teeth will do when the cutting time is over.

Therefore, babies use all the strength they have cutting first teeth. Some day in this venture they open their hands and lose the key. They do not realize that they can never get it back again and, therefore, will never catch a glimpse of the ships that sail on sunlit seas in fairy lands.

You, who have not cut your second teeth, come and play with us!

You, who are little children, come!

You, who are children still and do not know it, pretend that you are and tell us with your smiles that you can hear the echo of far-away youth sounding through the veils of leaves that have fallen in the years you have so seriously counted.

A PROLOGUE *exits at the right.* AN
ALIEN-KINSMAN *to the fairies, bearing
aloft a large globe of gold-fish, enters
from the left. As he appears he speaks
solemnly but with animation.*

An Alien-kinsman.   O Fiddlesticks!   I started
with the wrong toe!

*He turns, starts with the other foot,
crosses to the centre, places the globe
of gold-fish on the floor at the front of
the stage. He takes a peppermint
drop from the bag that hangs on a
cord from his arm, and presents it to
someone in the audience, then he draws
his index finger across his teeth three
times, for no reason at all—and exits
at the right.*

Reënter from the right A PROLOGUE, *who
points to the gentleman who has just
retired.*

A Prologue.   That, as you must surely know,

is an alien-kinsman to the fairies. He is peev-
ish with you and me because, by a spell of magic,
he has been transformed into half and half a
human being.

He is angry with you and with me because
neither you nor I had anything to do with his
transformation (which proves he is half human).

He sharpened his teeth at you,—that does not
mean he wants to eat you up.

He became very cross when you did not look
at him through opera glasses. There is nothing
that gives him so much delight as being looked
at through opera glasses (another proof of his
human nature).

I am sorry to have to inform you he will act
his trivial part in this play over and over again
until everyone pretends that he is looking at the
alien-kinsman of the fairies through opera glasses.

> A PROLOGUE *holds his hands to his eyes
> like opera glasses as a suggestion of
> what must be done and exits at the left.*

Reënter from the right AN ALIEN-KINSMAN
who crosses to the centre, takes up the
globe of gold-fish, and crosses to· the
left, then he turns and does it all over
again.

An Alien-kinsman.   O Fiddlesticks! I started
on the wrong toe.

He recrosses to the centre, again places
the globe of gold-fish in same spot,
presents peppermint to the same person,
and sharpens his teeth three times as
before.   As he retires he stops and
looks to see if everyone is pretending
to look at him through the opera
glasses.

If there is any one who does not enter into
his spirit of the play, he takes up the
gold-fish globe, turns and repeats in
detail his part until everyone pretends
to look at him through the glasses.
When that delightful thing is consum-

mated he smiles for the first time and exits at the right.

THE PLAY ITSELF

At the rise of the theatre curtain Robin Ringlet is discovered sitting in the first boat, with his hands clasping his knees, head thrown back, looking at a star which is directly overhead. After a moment or two he sings.

Robin Ringlet.   Ringlet, Ringlet,*
Wind a little stringlet,
Make a little swinglet
And swing, swing, swing.

Then without looking to right or left in a dreamy voice, he says:

The Loveliest Lady in the whole wide world plays games with me. She gave me a star for my very own, and she gave me a birthday. I like it more than I do my real birthday. On that day I do

*This is the song Mary Chickweed, the Seedwoman, sent to Robin Ringlet on his fourth birthday.

not know when I was born; it is pleasant to forget the date of your birth. In the sunshiny days of Springtime I can be sixteen and when Autumn has made the days gray I can be sixty. When you forget the exact date of your birth, it is as delightful to be sixty as sixteen. You do not feel you must at any time mind drafts, as all people do who know the hour, the day, the month, and the year of their birth. The Fairest lady presented me also with ninety-nine names and on my birthday she sent me ninety-nine gifts,—a present for every name. But on a day, once upon a time, my sweetest lady went away on a long, long journey. Before leaving, she took me into the park and put me into a little boat. It was a shell, blue inside and out, and once had been the house wherein a fish of some sort had lived in a warm Southern sea. She tied my boat to the North Star so I would not grow up while she was gone. And then she went away.

Here, I have waited for many long, lonely days, wishing for her to come back, drifting around and around the star to which my boat is tethered.

One day the Loveliest Lady sent me another little boat, a pearl-like shell from a far-away blue sea. I fastened it to the boat I am in and it is drifting in the wake my first boat is leaving in the water behind it.

Sometimes I am afraid the star to which my boat is tethered will set and take the boats and me into the dark places beyond the world.

Every evening I wish on the first star, that she would send me so many boats that they would stretch over the sea and all around the world until I came to the land where she is now.

Around and around the star I am drifting as the cow eats the grass in a ring around the tether in my Father's pasture.

Around and around the star the Loveliest Lady gave me, I am drifting, waiting for her to come back to play games with me.

He sings—

> Ringlet, Ringlet,
> Wind a little stringlet,
> Make a little swinglet,
> And swing, swing, swing.

Suddenly out of the wave at the prow of the first boat there appears upon adventure bent, a little nibbling nose.   It is a Sea-horse who sneezes three times.

Robin Ringlet (*somewhat taken back*).   You are a horse.

A Sea-horse (*stares at boy for a second*). Are you animal, mineral, or vegetable?

Robin Ringlet.   None, I am a boy.

A Sea-horse. (*Sneezes again three times.*)

Robin Ringlet (*positively*).   You *are* a horse.

A Sea-horse.   How did you know it?

Robin Ringlet.   You spit on me.   If horses sneeze when you are riding behind them, they always spit on you, and never say Excuse me. My Daddy said I must always say excuse me when I have to sneeze, and when any one else sneezes always say, God bless you.

A Sea-horse (jerks up his head and does as he is told).   Excuse me.

Robin Ringlet.   God bless you.

A Sea-horse.   My mother and father went away when I was a colt.   I never had any one to tell me what to say.   They only said "Gee-up" and "Whoa".   I'll do everything your Daddy told you to do if you will tell me.

Robin Ringlet.   Promise?

A Sea-horse.   Cross my heart and spit three times.

Robin Ringlet.   I think it was awful for your mother to leave you.

A Sea-horse.   It was not.   My father was a jumper and my mother can make a mile in one minute eleven and one-fifth seconds.   (*He neighs, and rears upright with pride.*)   I am going to be a circus horse when I grow up; a Mermaid with a pink and gold tail will ride on my back. She will swim right through hoops and rings, too. What are you going to be when you are a man?

Robin Ringlet. Sea Captain. I am going to have an albatross and a star tattooed on my left arm and on my right arm I will have L. L. inclosed within a circle. Everyone will know L. L. stands for Loveliest Lady. I'm going to have a two-bladed bone-handled knife. My ship will be a three-master with seventy guns, and the cabin will be packed brim full of raspberry jam. I'll have a line of brass cannon all along the deck. My men will fire every time I give the order. I'll sail across the Pacific and hunt for sharks and whales and icebergs. I'll bring a ship load of sea-shells and parrot's feathers and smelly flowers to my loveliest lady. And I won't ever part my hair in the middle. Don't you hate to have your hair brushed?

A Sea-horse. Never had it brushed. Nobody ever told me to.

Robin Ringlet. Nobody? Not even your nurse?

A Sea-horse. Never had a nurse.

Robin Ringlet. It must be fine when you don't have to be held by the chin and have your hair brushed and brushed and brushed. It is not so bad when they let you do it yourself. You don't have to hold your own chin tight to keep your head still.

A Sea-horse. Why do your have it brushed if you don't like it?

Robin Ringlet. Because if I don't, I shall get a cowlick.

A Sea-horse. Do horses have cowlicks?

Robin Ringlet. I don't know.

> A SEA-HORSE *laughs, but no one would ever have known it for Sea-horses never let any one see them laugh. It is not good breeding.*

A Sea-horse. A mackerel told me that all horses have to be curry-combed every morning and every night.   I can't imagine how it feels, but if your Daddy says it is right, why, then it must be elegant and genteel.   Did your Daddy say that all fine horses have to have their tails docked?

Robin Ringlet.   No, he did not say anything about tails.

> ROBIN RINGLET *and* A SEA-HORSE *are thoughtful.   Then* A SEA-HORSE *points with his nose to the figurehead on the first boat.*

A Sea-horse.   What is that?

Robin Ringlet.   Figurehead.

A Sea-horse.   What's a figurehead?

Robin Ringlet (*with an air of superior wisdom*).   A figurehead is an ornamental image on the prow of a vessel.

A Sea-horse.   What is yours?

Robin Ringlet.   Peacock's feather.

A Sea-Horse.   Why do you have that?

Robin Ringlet.   Because it has an eye.

A Sea-Horse.   It is only a feather one.

Robin Ringlet. But it has an eye just the same. Nearly everything you learn comes through your eyes.

A Sea-horse. It can't see.

Robin Ringlet. It can't see, it can't wink, and it doesn't cry. It is the only sort of eye that can look straight into the face of the Sun and never blink once.

A Sea-horse. A needle's eye doesn't blink.

Robin Ringlet. It doesn't blink because it's always stuffed full of thread.

A Sea-horse (is slightly puzzled). What does it mean?

Robin Ringlet. It means it is an honest, straightforward boat. That is the only sort of boat my loveliest lady would leave me in. Her heart is brimming over with beautiful thoughts. She can think the loveliest things and play the nicest games.

A Sea-horse (sniffs and proudly displays his wider knowledge of water information). This is

not a thought and it is not a game.   It is a dream
that keeps you from growing up.   It is a dream in
which you can play and play and play, for as long
as you pretend you will not grow up, you won't.

Robin Ringlet (*earnestly*).   Is it a really truly
really dream?

A Sea-horse (*smiles and nods slightly*).   True
as blue.

Robin Ringlet.   Of all the ladies in the whole
wide world only my lovely lady would think to
leave me in a little shell that has turned into a
dream.   I love dreams.   My Daddy has told me
that he feels I am safe when I am in a dream.   I
am so happy.   Mother and Daddy know I am
safe now because I am dreaming.   Maybe they
are standing by my bed and can see how happy
and safe I am.

A Sea-horse.   Dreams, you know, leave wakes
behind them as well as boats.   Wakes are heaps
and heaps of small bubbles and the bubbles that
form the wake of a dream are full of wonder,

beauty, and delight.   It is as nice to follow in the wake of a dream as it is to be in the dream itself.

> *This unwonted philosophy goes suddenly to* A SEA-HORSE'S *head.   He instantly becomes a Reformer and starts finding fault with poor* ROBIN RINGLET *on the instant.*

You are a selfish boy because you have no one riding in the boat that is following in the wake of your dream.   I do not play with selfish people. I will not have anything to do with them.   (*He neighs with scorn.*)   Good-day, selfish Robin Ringlet.

> *He disappears, the curl of his vanishing tail expressing utter indifference to everything on boats or land.*

Robin Ringlet.   Sea-horse, Sea-horse, Whoa! Whoa!   Please don't swim away.   I'll be unselfish.   I'll try my best to be unselfish.   Oh, he has gone away and left me.

He looks around, heaves a deep sigh,
pauses, then sighs again more heavily
than before and says sadly:

My dream is not so nice now.

Leaning over the side of the boat, and
holding his hand like a cup he brings
up some bubbles, which he throws into
the air, and quotes:

"Whatever goes up is obliged to come down,
Either on your head or either on the ground."

But ROBIN *finds that this is not much of*
a game to play when a little boy is
lonely, so he cries out:

It is not any fun when there is not anybody's
head for it to fall on!

Again he leans over the side of the boat,
but brings up only one bubble this
time and opens it joyfully.   Out of it
he takes a white feather from a bird's
wing but all he could think about was:

If the Sea-horse had waited, I would have been

willing to say I was wrong, as a man should. I
am a selfish boy. But Daddy said I must not
blubber.

> *He stands and looks around the horizon*
> *then up to the star, then thoughtfully*
> *at the feather. The star gives him*
> *an idea. He picks up his cap from*
> *the bottom of the boat and puts it on*
> *and makes the wish that will add*
> *this feather to it. He starts out fast*
> *enough and ends in a rapid jumble:*

"Star light, Star bright,

First star I have seen to-night,

I wish I may, I wish I might

Have the wish I have wished to-night."

(*Then he calls out loud*): Somebody! Somebody! Somebody! Please come and follow in
the wake of my dream. And make me an unselfish boy!

> *From the rear of the audience comes a*
> *boy who calls to him.*

Davy.   Hello!

Robin Ringlet.   Hio, Hi-o!

> *Now that he has proved to himself that he is no longer selfish,* ROBIN *gaily sticks the feather in his cap.*
>
> DAVY *comes up on the stage, pauses with wonder before the picture, looks curiously into the gold-fish globe, and he sticks his finger into the water.*

Robin Ringlet.   Get into the boat that is following in the wake of my dream.

> *As* DAVY *steps into the second boat his coat drops off, revealing him in clothes like* ROBIN RINGLET. *The coat falls over the frame partly inside and partly out of the picture.*

Robin Ringlet (turns and faces DAVY*).*   What is your name?

Davy. (out of breath from the long journey out of the audience into a dream).   Davy.   What is yours?

Robin Ringlet. Robin Ringlet. Have you any nick-names?

Davy (sadly). They used to call me Little Boy. But no one does any more.

Robin Ringlet. Why not?

Davy (bitterly). They thought I was no longer a little boy, and so they said I did not need it. Have you any names besides Robin?

Robin Ringlet (with pride). Ninety-nine; I would give you one of them if I could. But the Loveliest Lady in the whole wide world gave them to me. I could not part with one of them for anything. Davy, I will call you Little Boy and we can play and play. I'll let you make a wish on my first star. There it is. (*Pointing straight overhead*).

Davy. I wish——

Robin Ringlet (interrupting). You must not tell your wish or it will not come true. On my star you may make only a wish for your Mother. Look at the star. Then kiss the palm of your left hand. Blow the kiss to your Mother and say—"Star light, Star bright."

Davy (*kisses the palm of his left hand, places his left hand over his heart, after blowing a milk-weed seed into the audience*). A wish for my Mother:

"Star light, Star bright,

First star I've seen to-night,

I wish I may, I wish I might,

Have the wish I wish to-night."

(*He looks at the star longingly.*) Oh, I hope it will come true.

Robin Ringlet. I do, too.

Davy. Can you say all of your ninety-nine names?

Robin Ringlet (*with pride*). Yes, and I can say the English Kings. Can you?

Davy. No, I can't say all the kings of England but I can say the books of the Bible. (*With sing-song expression.*) Genesis, Exodus, Leviticus, Numbers, Deuter-ron——

But how could he keep his mind on the

books of the Bible when there were so many questions of his own that he wanted to ask? So he stopped suddenly and demanded:

What port are we sailing for?

Robin Ringlet. We are not sailing. We are drifting around and around a star to which our boats are tethered.

Davy. I thought we were sailing for San Salvador, China, and Peru to hunt in caves for pirates and hidden treasures.

Robin Ringlet. The boats are fastened to the North Star. We are drifting around and around, dreaming and dreaming in a world where we can sail anywhere we like.

Davy. I want to go to the South Pole.

Robin Ringlet. You cannot. Jack Frost will nip off your nose, my Loveliest Lady will not love you unless you have a nose.

Davy. If I did not have a nose, *they* would not keep saying to me, "Don't Sniffle."

Robin Ringlet.   You will have to follow in the white path of bubbles my boat is leaving in the water behind it.   I am going to sail into the Torrid Zone to hunt for heathen and cannibals. As soon as I can catch one I am going to cross the Atlantic, and bring a ship load of fruits and flowers to my Loveliest Lady.

Davy (*delighted*).   Can I bring her one?

Robin Ringlet.   A heathen, a fruit, a cannibal, or a flower.

Davy.   Orange.   Isn't it funny you don't have to see her to love her?

Robin Ringlet.   You can bring her an orange if you obey all my orders.

Davy.   But I am the captain of this boat. Whom will I order?

Robin Ringlet.   Nobody.   You are the captain of one of the boats that makes my Dream Fleet. The Loveliest Lady gave me all the boats.   She put me in this one so I could not grow up.

Davy.   Have you seen any whales?

Robin Ringlet. No. But I saw a Sea-horse. He told me it was not a really truly boat I am drifting in, but a ship that is in a dream. Dreams leave wakes behind them as well as boats. The Sea-horse said I was a selfish boy because I did not ask any one to follow in the wake of my dream. In the bubbles of the path in which your boat will sail there are gifts to you from the fairies. Here is one.

ROBIN *takes one bubble from the water.*

Oh! Inside of it, there is a *nut.*

This is a nut that grew on a tree where nuts usually grow. There is a squirrel in the park waiting for this very nut. When he comes and takes it out of your hand, you will know that you are being introduced to Sir Christopher Squirrel.

Davy (delighted). Can I have one?

Robin Ringlet. They are all for you, Little Boy.

Davy (takes a bubble). In this one there is an *acorn cup.* What does it mean?

Robin Ringlet. It means that sometime you

will be very thirsty. Someone will give you, no, not a chocolate ice cream soda, as I believe you are thinking, no,—a cup of cold water. It will be the sweetest drink you have ever had.

Davy. How can you tell what they mean?

Robin Ringlet (fumbling in his coat pocket). I have sea-weed seed. When you have sea-weed seed in the pocket that is right over your heart, you can understand fish-talk and you can sing the songs that are inside of bubbles.

Davy. I wish I had some. I will give you an agate and three chinies for some.

Robin Ringlet. I will not sell them. If you obey all the orders given by the Rear Admiral Commodore Adjutant General L. L. D. F., I might give you some.

Davy (in awe). Are you a Rear Comy-dore, Gen-ral——

Robin Ringlet (stands, turns, and faces DAVY). Rear Admiral, Commodore Adjutant General L. L. D. F.

Davy.   What is L. L. D. F?

Robin Ringlet (shakes a warning finger). Loveliest Lady's Dream Fleet.

Davy (salutes).   O!   I'll obey all your orders, Rear Admiral Commodore General Robin Ringlet L. L. D. F., and I'll give you my agate, too.

Robin Ringlet (salutes).   Thanks, Captain Davy Littleboy.   Stand up!—Don't shake the boat!— Sit down.

Davy (obeys the orders).   What can we do to make it last out?

Robin Ringlet.   I don't want it to last out. As soon as it is over my Loveliest Lady will come back.

Davy.   What else did the Sea-horse say?

Robin Ringlet.   He told me what he was going to be and I told him what I was going to be.

Davy.   What are you going to be?

Robin Ringlet (with dignity). Sea Captain.

Davy.   I am going to be a Major General.

My father was a Major and Mother said, if I do all my long divisions, she will give me his sword one day.

Robin Ringlet. Where is your Mother?

Davy (*pointing*). There, fourth row, centre. (*when he sees his Mother*) I wish I could take her one bubble.

Robin Ringlet (*looks for* DAVY'S *Mother; finds her and smiles*). You can, if you will come back. You can take her two bubbles. Take heaps and heaps. Take as many as you can carry and come back and get some more.

DAVY *fills his arms full.*

Robin Ringlet. Can't you carry more than that? Stuff your pockets full, stuff them in your shirt. Fill your hat full. Why didn't you bring a hat that would hold water?

With his arms full of bubbles, DAVY *steps out of the boat over the picture frame to the fore-stage.*

Robin Ringlet (*standing*). Halt! Captain

Little Boy! About face! You cannot sing the songs that are inside of bubbles unless you have sea-weed seed in your pocket.

> ROBIN *puts some seed into* DAVY'S *pocket.*

Davy. Thanks, Robin.

Robin Ringlet. Thank you, Little Boy! I am not selfish!

> *Looks beyond the audience, as though he were searching the horizon for a ship that will bring back the Loveliest Lady.*
>
> *As* DAVY *turns away from the picture, the curtain falls behind him, hiding the two boats and leaving him with his arms full of bubbles. He places the bubbles in a pile near the gold-fish globe. When he discovers the audience again, for he has forgotten all about them, he spreads his arms with delight. He takes one of the bubbles and from it he draws a* WHITE FEATHER *saying, as he presents it to someone in the audience.*

Davy. This is a feather from a Mother bird's wing. It signifies that soon your dear Mother will take you in her lap, you will lay your head on her arm and sleep. It will be so sweet you will not know you are asleep.

> *He comes back to the pile of bubbles, takes another which he presents to someone, and still another, until he has given away all of them.*
>
> *Within the bubbles are hidden the following gifts:*

Seven Sunflower Seeds—

Goldfinches are cousins to the fairies, twice removed on their Mother's side. They are very fond of sunflower seed. Plant these seeds in a garden and give the goldfinches a dinner. For your kindness to their relatives, the fairies will reward you with good fortune.

Snail's Shell—

This is a snail's house. When a snail goes on a

journey, he carries his house with him packed on his back.   If he grows weary he crawls into his house and takes a nap.   It signifies: "Soon you will go on a long, slow journey."

Pressed Pansy—

This little flower raised its head out of Robin Ringlet's blue bowl.   It said, "Give me the sweetest gift you have."   The nicest gift I have to give the little flower is that it comes to live with you.

Blue Bag of White Stones—

If you are walking in the woods and suddenly feel you are going to get lost, drop these pebbles in your path.   When you are lost, they will lead you home.

A Seed Ball from a Sweet Gum Tree—

This is a ball that grew on a tree where balls do not usually grow.   It is a charm to prevent those people looking at you who stare and glare. Show them this ball when they gaze at you, immediately they will stop staring and look at the sky.

A Sea-shell—

The next time you go into the water to swim, open your eyes wide. A little fish will come there as a messenger from the mermaids to see the colour of your eyes. Instead of poster-stamps and post-cards, Mermaids collect the colours of eyes. They wish to add your eyes to their collection and write their colour on the white sands on the bottom of the sea.

A Button—

This is a button from a beggar man's coat; "Rich man, Poor man, Beggar man—" I will not say thief. What do you wish to be when you grow up instead of a thief?

The Inner Lining of the Seed-pod of Shepherd's Purse, (also called honesty or poor man's money)—

This is not a fairy's wing as you think it is, although it is like the wings on which fairies fly.

When you hold it between your eyes and the light it is like a star shining through a cloud. Place it in your pocket and when you see a star reflected in the water of a lake you will know the fairies are near.

An Empty Spool—

If you have a wish to send to the fairies, blow it into a bubble through this spool. Send the bubble out of the window on a night when the moon is full.

The Cone from a Cedar Tree—

This is a cone that fell from a tree on which berries grow. Birthday candles are made from the wax of the berries. It signifies " The next birthday will be the nicest you have ever had."

Please ask ROBIN and DAVID to your party.

A Bean—

This is a bean. It did not grow on Jack's stalk, it came out of the sea. In many ways it is superior to Jack's beans. If you meet a giant walking down a road, rub it on your forehead three times. Suddenly the giant will "about face" and walk off in the opposite direction.

A Feather from a Guinea-fowl—

Should there be reported in your neighbour-hood the news of the arrival of those naughty creatures that make you speckled like a guinea-hen, I mean Mr. Measles, or Mrs. Freckles, or Charlie Chicken-pox, hold this feather over your hand, thus. Maybe they will think you are properly speckled and pass you by.

A Feather from a Canary Bird's Wing—

This is a feather from the wing of a little bird named Mose. His mamma trims his claws once a week. The perches in his cage are not rough like the branches of trees, and so they do not manicure his nails in proper Canary fashion. It signifies: "When you grow up you will have a rising moon in every finger-tip." I have two just coming up on my thumbs.

Autumn-leaf—

This is a leaf that has danced down the autumn breezes. With it comes this wish from the fairies,—"When you dance may you feel as 'dancy' as a falling leaf." Pan said: "Nothing is quite so dancy."

Lucky-penny—

This signifies good fortune to you from the fairies and from ROBIN RINGLET.

A Long White Feather—

This is a feather from a large bird's wing. Should you come to the little gate that will not open, stick the feather behind your left ear, fold your arms, and sing the rhyme Mary Chickweed, the Seed-woman, sent to ROBIN RINGLET on his fourth birthday, then put the feather into the keyhole and the little gate will open.

A Daffodil—

This is a flower for the child born on **Sunday**.

"The child that is born on the Sabbath day,
Is bright and bonny, blithe and gay."

A green feather from a parrot's wing—

This is a feather from a parrot who sat in a golden ring and said: "Columbia the Gem of the Ocean." He plucked one feather from his wing and said: "I send this feather to a little girl named Elizabeth."

> *When* DAVY *has given out the last bubble gift, he returns to them as though he expects to find more. When he discovers there are no bubbles left, he starts to go back into the dream. He finds the curtain shutting out the dream and turns suddenly.*

Davy. ROBIN RINGLET has left me, and I have strayed out of the wake of his dream. There is not a bubble from the fairies left for my Mother. Will not someone give me a gift to take to my Mother? (*As someone in the audi-*

ence returns one of the gifts given by Davy.) No, never mind, I wanted to know if you were unselfish like Robin Ringlet; keep your gift, I will carry the gold-fish to her. (*He takes up the globe of gold-fish and looks at the audience over it.*) You thought I was not in this play. You thought I belonged out there in the audience. I have fooled you. I AM in the play. Goodbye, audience.

> *He then retires between the curtains, singing:*
> "Ringlet, Ringlet,
>   Wind a little stringlet,
>   Make a little swinglet
>   And swing, swing, swing."
>
> *And if the audience has been a real audience, it has been in the play, too.*

THE END

THE COUNTRY LIFE PRESS
GARDEN CITY, N. Y.

Lightning Source UK Ltd.
Milton Keynes UK
UKHW021847240722
406312UK00003B/17

9 780342 952472